P9-EDZ-636

WODWO

TED HUGHES

WODWO

FABER AND FABER

3 Queen Square

London

CAMROSE LUTHERAN COLLEGE
LIBRARY

First published in 1967
by Faber and Faber Limited
3 Queen Square London WC1
First published in this edition 1971
Reprinted 1972
Printed in Great Britain
by Latimer Trend & Co Ltd Whitstable
All rights reserved

ISBN 0 571 09714 6 (Faber Paper Covered Edition)

PR
6058
.U37
W6
1967 /49,151

© 1967 by Ted Hughes

CONDITIONS OF SALE

This book is sold subject to the condition that it shall not, by way of
trade or otherwise, be lent, re-sold, hired out or otherwise circulated
without the publisher's prior consent in any form of binding or cover
other than that in which it is published and without a similar condi-
tion including this condition being imposed on the subsequent purchaser

To my Mother and Father

Author's Note

The stories and the play in this book may be read as notes, appendix and unversified episodes of the events behind the poems, or as chapters of a single adventure to which the poems are commentary and amplification. Either way, the verse and the prose are intended to be read together, as parts of a single work.

Contents

PART I

PART II

PART III

Sumwhyle wyth wormeʒ he werreʒ, and wyth wolves als,
Sumwhyle wyth wodwos, þat woned in þe knarreʒ,
Boþe wyth bulleʒ and bereʒ, and boreʒ oþerquyle,
And etayneʒ, þat hym anelede of þe heʒe felle.

Sir Gawayn And Þe Grene Knyʒt, lines 720–724

PART I

Thistles

Against the rubber tongues of cows and the hoeing
   hands of men
Thistles spike the summer air
Or crackle open under a blue-black pressure.

Every one a revengeful burst
Of resurrection, a grasped fistful
Of splintered weapons and Icelandic frost thrust up

From the underground stain of a decayed Viking.
They are like pale hair and the gutturals of dialects.
Every one manages a plume of blood.

Then they grow grey, like men.
Mown down, it is a feud. Their sons appear,
Stiff with weapons, fighting back over the same ground.

Still Life

Outcrop stone is miserly

With the wind. Hoarding its nothings,
Letting wind run through its fingers,
It pretends to be dead of lack.
Even its grimace is empty,
Warted with quartz pebbles from the sea's womb.

It thinks it pays no rent,
Expansive in the sun's summerly reckoning.
Under rain, it gleams exultation blackly
As if receiving interest.
Similarly, it bears the snow well.

Wakeful and missing little and landmarking
The fly-like dance of the planets,
The landscape moving in sleep,
It expects to be in at the finish.
Being ignorant of this other, this harebell,

That trembles, as under threats of death,
In the summer turf's heat-rise,
And in which—filling veins
Any known name of blue would bruise
Out of existence—sleeps, recovering,

The maker of the sea.

Her Husband

Comes home dull with coal-dust deliberately
To grime the sink and foul towels and let her
Learn with scrubbing brush and scrubbing board
The stubborn character of money.

And let her learn through what kind of dust
He has earned his thirst and the right to quench it
And what sweat he has exchanged for his money
And the blood-weight of money. He'll humble her

With new light on her obligations.
The fried, woody chips, kept warm two hours in the oven,
Are only part of her answer.
Hearing the rest, he slams them to the fire back

And is away round the house-end singing
'Come back to Sorrento' in a voice
Of resounding corrugated iron.
Her back has bunched into a hump as an insult.

For they will have their rights.
Their jurors are to be assembled
From the little crumbs of soot. Their brief
Goes straight up to heaven and nothing more is heard of it.

Cadenza

The violinist's shadow vanishes.

The husk of a grasshopper
Sucks a remote cyclone and rises.

The full, bared throat of a woman walking water,
The loaded estuary of the dead.

And I am the cargo
Of a coffin attended by swallows.

And I am the water
Bearing the coffin that will not be silent.

The clouds are full of surgery and collisions
But the coffin escapes—as a black diamond,

A ruby brimming blood,
An emerald beating its shores,

The sea lifts swallow wings and flings
A summer lake open,

Sips and bewilders its reflection,
Till the whole sky dives shut like a burned land back to its
    spark—

A bat with a ghost in its mouth
Struck at by lightnings of silence—

Blue with sweat, the violinist
Crashes into the orchestra, which explodes.

Ghost Crabs

At nightfall, as the sea darkens,
A depth darkness thickens, mustering from the gulfs and the
submarine badlands,
To the sea's edge. To begin with
It looks like rocks uncovering, mangling their pallor.
Gradually the labouring of the tide
Falls back from its productions,
Its power slips back from glistening nacelles, and they are
crabs.
Giant crabs, under flat skulls, staring inland
Like a packed trench of helmets.
Ghosts, they are ghost-crabs.
They emerge
An invisible disgorging of the sea's cold
Over the man who strolls along the sands.
They spill inland, into the smoking purple
Of our woods and towns—a bristling surge
Of tall and staggering spectres
Gliding like shocks through water.
Our walls, our bodies, are no problem to them.
Their hungers are homing elsewhere.
We cannot see them or turn our minds from them.
Their bubbling mouths, their eyes
In a slow mineral fury
Press through our nothingness where we sprawl on our beds,
Or sit in our rooms. Our dreams are ruffled maybe.
Or we jerk awake to the world of our possessions
With a gasp, in a sweat burst, brains jamming blind
Into the bulb-light. Sometimes, for minutes, a sliding
Staring
Thickness of silence
Presses between us. These crabs own this world.

All night, around us or through us,
They stalk each other, they fasten on to each other,
They mount each other, they tear each other to pieces,
They utterly exhaust each other.
They are the powers of this world.
We are their bacteria,
Dying their lives and living their deaths.
At dawn, they sidle back under the sea's edge.
They are the turmoil of history, the convulsion
In the roots of blood, in the cycles of concurrence.
To them, our cluttered countries are empty battleground. ·
All day they recuperate under the sea.
Their singing is like a thin sea-wind flexing in the rocks of
a headland,
Where only crabs listen.

They are God's only toys.

Boom

And faces at the glutted shop-windows
Gaze into the bottomless well
Of wishes

Like rearlights away up the long road
Toward an earth-melting dawn
Of the same thing, but staler.

More More More
Meaning Air Water Life
Cry the mouths

That are filling with burning ashes.

Ludwig's Death Mask

Words for his ugly mug his
Naked exhibitions at windows shaking a
Fist at the gapers, his whalish appetite
For cold douches and changing lodgings.

Words for his black-mouth derisive
Engulfing in laughter the sweet-eyed attendance
Of aesthetes spreading their marzipan amazement
Over his music and nibbling it amazedly off.

But no words for the loyal
Formations of angels which attended
All this in misunderstanding and
Despair and finally grimly as Shakespeare

Caused himself flee seventeen feet down
Through the church-floor into dumb earth touched
His ears dead to continue complete
In union with the communion of angels.

Second Glance at a Jaguar

Skinfull of bowls, he bowls them,
The hip going in and out of joint, dropping the spine
With the urgency of his hurry
Like a cat going along under thrown stones, under cover,
Glancing sideways, running
Under his spine. A terrible, stump-legged waddle
Like a thick Aztec disemboweller,
Club-swinging, trying to grind some square
Socket between his hind legs round,
Carrying his head like a brazier of spilling embers,
And the black bit of his mouth, he takes it
Between his back teeth, he has to wear his skin out,
He swipes a lap at the water-trough as he turns,
Swivelling the ball of his heel on the polished spot,
Showing his belly like a butterfly,
At every stride he has to turn a corner
In himself and correct it. His head
Is like the worn down stump of another whole jaguar,
His body is just the engine shoving it forward,
Lifting the air up and shoving on under,
The weight of his fangs hanging the mouth open,
Bottom jaw combing the ground. A gorged look,
Gangster, club-tail lumped along behind gracelessly,
He's wearing himself to heavy ovals,
Muttering some mantrah, some drum-song of murder
To keep his rage brightening, making his skin
Intolerable, spurred by the rosettes, the cain-brands,
Wearing the spots off from the inside,
Rounding some revenge. Going like a prayer-wheel,
The head dragging forward, the body keeping up,

The hind legs lagging. He coils, he flourishes
The blackjack tail as if looking for a target,
Hurrying through the underworld, soundless.

Public Bar TV

On a flaked ridge of the desert

Outriders have found foul water. They say nothing;
With the cactus and the petrified tree
Crouch numbed by a wind howling all
Visible horizons equally empty.

The wind brings dust and nothing
Of the wives, the children, the grandmothers
With the ancestral bones, who months ago
Left the last river,

Coming at the pace of oxen.

Fern

Here is the fern's frond, unfurling a gesture,
Like a conductor whose music will now be pause
And the one note of silence
To which the whole earth dances gravely.

The mouse's ear unfurls its trust,
The spider takes up her bequest,
And the retina
Reins the creation with a bridle of water.

And, among them, the fern
Dances gravely, like the plume
Of a warrior returning, under the low hills,

Into his own kingdom.

A Wind Flashes the Grass

Leaves pour blackly across.
We cling to the earth, with glistening eyes, pierced afresh
                                by the tree's cry.

And the incomprehensible cry
From the boughs, in the wind
Sets us listening for below words,
Meanings that will not part from the rock.

The trees thunder in unison, on a gloomy afternoon,
And the ploughman grows anxious, his tractor becomes
    terrible,
As his memory litters downwind
And the shadow of his bones tosses darkly on the air.

The trees suddenly storm to a stop in a hush
Against the sky, where the field ends.
And crowd there shuddering
And wary, like horses bewildered by lightning.

The stirring of their twigs against the dark, travelling sky
Is the oracle of the earth

They too are afraid they too are momentary
Streams rivers of shadow.

A Vegetarian

Fearful of the hare with the manners of a lady,
Of the sow's loaded side and the boar's brown fang,

Fearful of the bull's tongue snaring and rending,
And of the sheep's jaw moving without mercy,

Tripped on Eternity's stone threshold.

                        Staring into the emptiness,
Unable to move, he hears the hounds of the grass.

Sugar Loaf

The trickle cutting from the hill-crown
Whorls to a pure pool here, with a whisp trout like a spirit.
The water is wild as alcohol—
Distilling from the fibres of the blue wind.
Reeds, nude and tufted, shiver as they wade.

I see the whole huge hill in the small pool's stomach.

This will be serious for the hill.
It suspects nothing.
Crammed with darkness, the dull, trusting giant
Leans, as over a crystal, over the water
Where his future is forming.

Bowled Over

By kiss of death, bullet on brow,
No more life can overpower
That first infatuation, world cannot
Ever be harder or clearer or come
Closer than when it arrived there

Spinning its patched fields, churches,
Trees where nightingales sang in broad daylight
And vast flaring blue skirts of seas—
Then sudden insubordination
Of boredom and sleep

When the eyes could not find their keys
Or the neck remember what mother whispered
Or the body stand to its word.

Desertion in the face of a bullet!

Buried without honours.

Wino

Grape is my mulatto mother
In this frozen whited country. Her veined interior
Hangs hot open for me to re-enter
The blood-coloured glasshouse against which the stone
   world
Thins to a dew and steams off—
Diluting neither my blood cupful
Nor its black undercurrent. I swell in there, soaking.
Till the grape for sheer surfeit of me
Vomits me up. I'm found
Feeble as a babe, but renewed.

Logos

God gives the blinding pentagram of His power
For the frail mantle of a person
To be moulded onto. So if they come
This unlikely far, and against such odds—
                    the perfect strength is God's.

And if the family features mount yet another
Opportune, doomed bid
To grapple to everlasting
Their freehold of life—
                    it is by God's leave.

Creation convulses in nightmare. And awaking
Suddenly tastes the nightmare moving
Still in its mouth
And spits it kicking out, with a swinish cry—
                    which is God's first cry.

Like that cry within the sea,
A mumbling over and over
Of ancient law, the phrasing falling to pieces
Garbled among shell-shards and gravels,
                    the truths falling to pieces,

The sea pulling everything to pieces
Except its killers, alert and shapely.
And within seconds the new-born baby is lamenting
That it ever lived—
          God is a good fellow, but His mother's against Him.

Reveille

No, the serpent was not
One of God's ordinary creatures.
Where did he creep from,
This legless land-swimmer with a purpose?

Adam and lovely Eve
Deep in the first dream
Each the everlasting
Holy One of the other

Woke with cries of pain.
Each clutched a throbbing wound—
A sudden, cruel bite.
The serpent's head, small and still,

Smiled under the lilies.
Behind him, his coils
Had crushed all Eden's orchards.
And out beyond Eden

The black, thickening river of his body
Glittered in giant loops
Around desert mountains and away
Over the ashes of the future.

The Rescue

That's what we live on: thinking of their rescue
And fitting our future to it. You have to see it:
First, the dry smudge above the sea-line,
Then the slow growth of a shipful of strangers
Into this existence. White bows, the white bow-wave
Cleaving the nightmare, slicing it open,
Letting in reality. Then all the sailors white
As maggots waving at the rail. Then their shouting—
Faintly at first, as you can think
The crowd coming with Christ sounded
To Lazarus in his cave.
Then the ship's horn giving blast after blast out
Announcing the end of the island. Then the rowboat.
I fancy I saw it happen. The five were standing
In the shallows with the deathly sea
Lipping their knees and the rattle of oar-locks
Shaking the sand out of their brain-cells,
The flash of wet oars slashing their eyes back alive—
All the time the long white liner anchoring the world
Just out there, crowded and watching.
Then there came a moment in the eternity of this island
When the rowboat's bows bit into the beach
And the lovely greetings and chatter scattered—
This is wrong.
        The five never moved.
They just stood sucked empty
As grasses by this island's silence. And the crew
Helped them into the boat not speaking
Knowing the sound of a voice from the world
Might grab too cheery-clumsy
Into their powdery nerves. Then they rowed off
Toward the shining ship with carefully

Hushed oars dipping and squeaking. And the five sat all the
   time
Like mummies with their bandages lifted off—
While the ship's dazzling side brimmed up the sky
And leaned over, pouring faces.

Stations

I

Suddenly his poor body
Had its drowsy mind no longer
For insulation.

Before the funeral service foundered
The lifeboat coffin had shaken to pieces
And the great stars were swimming through where he had
  been.

For a while

The stalk of the tulip at the door that had outlived him,
And his jacket, and his wife, and his last pillow
Clung to each other.

II

I can understand the haggard eyes
Of the old

Dry wrecks

Broken by seas of which they could drink nothing.

III

You are a wild look—out of an egg
Laid by your absence.

In the great Emptiness you sit complacent,
Blackbird in wet snow.

If you could make only one comparison—
Your condition is miserable, you would give up.

But you, from the start, surrender to total Emptiness,
Then leave everything to it.

Absence. It is your own
Absence

Weeps its respite through your accomplished music,
Wraps its cloak dark about your feeding.

IV

Whether you say it, think it, know it
Or not, it happens, it happens, as
Over rails over
The neck the wheels leave
The head with its vocabulary useless,
Among the flogged plantains.

The Green Wolf

Your neighbour moves less and less, attempts less.
If his right hand still moves, it is a farewell
Already days posthumous.

But the left hand seems to freeze,
And the left leg with its crude plumbing,
And the left half jaw and the left eyelid and the words,
                                        all the huge cries

Frozen in his brain his tongue cannot unfreeze—
While somewhere through a dark heaven
The dark bloodclot moves in.

You watch it approaching but you cannot fear it.
The punctual evening star,
Worse, the warm hawthorn blossoms, their foam,

Their palls of deathly perfume,
Worst of all the beanflower
Badged with jet like the ear of the tiger

Unmake and remake you. That star
And that flower and that flower
And living mouth and living mouth all

One smouldering annihilation
Of old brains, old bowels, old bodies
In the scarves of dew, the wet hair of nightfall.

The Bear

In the huge, wide-open, sleeping eye of the mountain
The bear is the gleam in the pupil
Ready to awake
And instantly focus.

The bear is glueing
Beginning to end
With glue from people's bones
In his sleep.

The bear is digging
In his sleep
Through the wall of the Universe
With a man's femur.

The bear is a well
Too deep to glitter
Where your shout
Is being digested.

The bear is a river
Where people bending to drink
See their dead selves.

The bear sleeps
In a kingdom of walls
In a web of rivers.

He is the ferryman
To dead land.

His price is everything.

PART II

The Rain Horse

As the young man came over the hill the first thin blowing of
rain met him. He turned his coat-collar up and stood on top
of the shelving rabbit-riddled hedgebank, looking down into
the valley.

He had come too far. What had set out as a walk along
pleasantly-remembered tarmac lanes had turned dreamily by
gate and path and hedge-gap into a cross-ploughland trek, his
shoes ruined, the dark mud of the lower fields inching up the
trouser legs of his grey suit where they rubbed against each
other. And now there was a raw, flapping wetness in the air
that would be downpour again at any minute. He shivered,
holding himself tense against the cold.

This was the view he had been thinking of. Vaguely, with-
out really directing his walk, he had felt he would get the
whole thing from this point. For twelve years, whenever he
had recalled this scene, he had imagined it as it looked from
here. Now the valley lay sunken in front of him, utterly
deserted, shallow, bare fields, black and sodden as the bed of
an ancient lake after the weeks of rain.

Nothing happened. Not that he had looked forward to any
very transfiguring experience. But he had expected some-
thing, some pleasure, some meaningful sensation, he didn't
quite know what.

So he waited, trying to nudge the right feelings alive with the
details—the surprisingly familiar curve of the hedges, the
stone gate-pillar and iron gatehook let into it that he had
used as a target, the long bank of the rabbit-warren on which

he stood and which had been the first thing he ever noticed about the hill when twenty years ago, from the distance of the village, he had said to himself 'That looks like rabbits'.

Twelve years had changed him. This land no longer recognized him, and he looked back at it coldly, as at a finally visited home-country, known only through the stories of a grandfather; felt nothing but the dullness of feeling nothing. Boredom. Then, suddenly, impatience, with a whole exasperated swarm of little anxieties about his shoes, and the spitting rain and his new suit and that sky and the two-mile trudge through the mud back to the road.

It would be quicker to go straight forward to the farm a mile away in the valley and behind which the road looped. But the thought of meeting the farmer—to be embarrassingly remembered or shouted at as a trespasser—deterred him. He saw the rain pulling up out of the distance, dragging its grey broken columns, smudging the trees and the farms.

A wave of anger went over him: anger against himself for blundering into this mud-trap and anger against the land that made him feel so outcast, so old and stiff and stupid. He wanted nothing but to get away from it as quickly as possibel. But as he turned, something moved in his eye-corner. All his senses startled alert. He stopped.

Over to his right a thin, black horse was running across the ploughland towards the hill, its head down, neck stretched out. It seemed to be running on its toes like a cat, like a dog up to no good.

From the high point on which he stood the hill dipped slightly and rose to another crested point fringed with the tops of trees, three hundred yards to his right. As he watched it, the horse ran up to that crest, showed against the sky— for a moment like a nightmarish leopard—and disappeared over the other side.

For several seconds he stared at the skyline, stunned by the unpleasantly strange impression the horse had made on him.

Then the plastering beat of icy rain on his bare skull brought him to himself. The distance had vanished in a wall of grey. All around him the fields were jumping and streaming.

Holding his collar close and tucking his chin down into it he ran back over the hilltop towards the town-side, the lee-side, his feet sucking and splashing, at every stride plunging to the ankle.

This hill was shaped like a wave, a gently rounded back lifting out of the valley to a sharply crested, almost concave front hanging over the river meadows towards the town. Down this front, from the crest, hung two small woods separated by a fallow field. The near wood was nothing more than a quarry, circular, full of stones and bracken, with a few thorns and nondescript saplings, foxholes and rabbit holes. The other was rectangular, mainly a planting of scrub oak trees. Beyond the river smouldered the town like a great heap of blue cinders.

He ran along the top of the first wood and finding no shelter but the thin, leafless thorns of the hedge, dipped below the crest out of the wind and jogged along through thick grass to the wood of oaks. In blinding rain he lunged through the barricade of brambles at the wood's edge. The little crippled trees were small choice in the way of shelter, but at a sudden fierce thickening of the rain he took one at random and crouched down under the leaning trunk.

Still panting from his run, drawing his knees up tightly, he watched the bleak lines of rain, grey as hail, slanting through the boughs into the clumps of bracken and bramble. He felt hidden and safe. The sound of the rain as it rushed and lulled in the wood seemed to seal him in. Soon the chilly sheet lead of his suit became a tight, warm mould, and gradually he sank into a state of comfort that was all but trance, though the rain beat steadily on his exposed shoulders and trickled down the oak trunk on to his neck.

All around him the boughs angled down, glistening, black

as iron. From their tips and elbows the drops hurried steadily, and the channels of the bark pulsed and gleamed. For a time he amused himself calculating the variation in the rainfall by the variations in a dribble of water from a trembling twig-end two feet in front of his nose. He studied the twig, bringing dwarfs and continents and animals out of its scurfy bark. Beyond the boughs the blue shoal of the town was rising and falling, and darkening and fading again, in the pale, swaying backdrop of rain.

He wanted this rain to go on forever. Whenever it seemed to be drawing off he listened anxiously until it closed in again. As long as it lasted he was suspended from life and time. He didn't want to return to his sodden shoes and his possibly ruined suit and the walk back over that land of mud.

All at once he shivered. He hugged his knees to squeeze out the cold and found himself thinking of the horse. The hair on the nape of his neck prickled slightly. He remembered how it had run up to the crest and showed against the sky.

He tried to dismiss the thought. Horses wander about the countryside often enough. But the image of the horse as it had appeared against the sky stuck in his mind. It must have come over the crest just above the wood in which he was now sitting. To clear his mind, he twisted around and looked up the wood between the tree stems, to his left.

At the wood top, with the silvered grey light coming in behind it, the black horse was standing under the oaks, its head high and alert, its ears pricked, watching him.

A horse sheltering from the rain generally goes into a sort of stupor, tilts a hind hoof and hangs its head and lets its eyelids droop, and so it stays as long as the rain lasts. This horse was nothing like that. It was watching him intently, standing perfectly still, its soaked neck and flank shining in the hard light.

He turned back. His scalp went icy and he shivered. What was he to do? Ridiculous to try driving it away. And to leave the wood, with the rain still coming down full pelt, was out of the question. Meanwhile the idea of being watched became more and more unsettling until at last he had to twist around again, to see if the horse had moved. It stood exactly as before.

This was absurd. He took control of himself and turned back deliberately, determined not to give the horse one more thought. If it wanted to share the wood with him, let it. If it wanted to stare at him, let it. He was nestling firmly into these resolutions when the ground shook and he heard the crash of a heavy body coming down the wood. Like lightning his legs bounded him upright and about face. The horse was almost on top of him, its head stretching forwards, ears flattened and lips lifted back from the long yellow teeth. He got one snapshot glimpse of the red-veined eyeball as he flung himself backwards around the tree. Then he was away up the slope, whipped by oak twigs as he leapt the brambles and brushwood, twisting between the close trees till he tripped and sprawled. As he fell the warning flashed through his head that he must at all costs keep his suit out of the leaf-mould, but a more urgent instinct was already rolling him violently sideways. He spun around, sat up and looked back, ready to scramble off in a flash to one side. He was panting from the sudden excitement and effort. The horse had disappeared. The wood was empty except for the drumming, slant grey rain, dancing the bracken and glittering from the branches.

He got up, furious. Knocking the dirt and leaves from his suit as well as he could he looked around for a weapon. The horse was evidently mad, had an abscess on its brain or something of the sort. Or maybe it was just spiteful. Rain sometimes puts creatures into queer states. Whatever it was, he was going to get away from the wood as quickly as possible, rain or no rain.

Since the horse seemed to have gone on down the wood, his way to the farm over the hill was clear. As he went, he broke a yard length of wrist-thick dead branch from one of the oaks, but immediately threw it aside and wiped the slime of rotten wet bark from his hands with his soaked handkerchief. Already he was thinking it incredible that the horse could have meant to attack him. Most likely it was just going down the wood for better shelter and had made a feint at him in passing—as much out of curiosity or playfulness as anything. He recalled the way horses menace each other when they are galloping around in a paddock.

The wood rose to a steep bank topped by the hawthorn hedge that ran along the whole ridge of the hill. He was pulling himself up to a thin place in the hedge by the bare stem of one of the hawthorns when he ducked and shrank down again. The swelling gradient of fields lay in front of him, smoking in the slowly crossing rain. Out in the middle of the first field, tall as a statue, and a ghostly silver in the undercloud light, stood the horse, watching the wood.

He lowered his head slowly, slithered back down the bank and crouched. An awful feeling of helplessness came over him. He felt certain the horse had been looking straight at him. Waiting for him? Was it clairvoyant? Maybe a mad animal can be clairvoyant. At the same time he was ashamed to find himself acting so inanely, ducking and creeping about in this way just to keep out of sight of a horse. He tried to imagine how anybody in their senses would just walk off home. This cooled him a little, and he retreated farther down the wood. He would go back the way he had come, along under the hill crest, without any more nonsense.

The wood hummed and the rain was a cold weight, but he observed this rather than felt it. The water ran down inside his clothes and squelched in his shoes as he eased his way carefully over the bedded twigs and leaves. At every instant he expected to see the prick-eared black head looking down at him from the hedge above.

At the woodside he paused, close against a tree. The success of this last manoeuvre was restoring his confidence, but he didn't want to venture out into the open field without making sure that the horse was just where he had left it. The perfect move would be to withdraw quietly and leave the horse standing out there in the rain. He crept up again among the trees to the crest and peeped through the hedge.

The grey field and the whole slope were empty. He searched the distance. The horse was quite likely to have forgotten him altogether and wandered off. Then he raised himself and leaned out to see if it had come in close to the hedge. Before he was aware of anything the ground shook. He twisted around wildly to see how he had been caught. The black shape was above him, right across the light. Its whinnying snort and the spattering whack of its hooves seemed to be actually inside his head as he fell backwards down the bank, and leapt again like a madman, dodging among the oaks, imagining how the buffet would come and how he would be knocked headlong. Half-way down the wood the oaks gave way to bracken and old roots and stony rabbit diggings. He was well out into the middle of this before he realized that he was running alone.

Gasping for breath now and cursing mechanically, without a thought for his suit he sat down on the ground to rest his shaking legs, letting the rain plaster the hair down over his forehead and watching the dense flashing lines disappear abruptly into the soil all around him as if he were watching through thick plate glass. He took deep breaths in the effort to steady his heart and regain control of himself. His right trouser turn-up was ripped at the seam and his suit jacket was splashed with the yellow mud of the top field.

Obviously the horse had been farther along the hedge above the steep field, waiting for him to come out at the woodside just as he had intended. He must have peeped through the hedge—peeping the wrong way—within yards of it.

However, this last attack had cleared up one thing. He need

no longer act like a fool out of mere uncertainty as to whether the horse was simply being playful or not. It was definitely after him. He picked up two stones about the size of goose eggs and set off towards the bottom of the wood, striding carelessly.

A loop of the river bordered all this farmland. If he crossed the little level meadow at the bottom of the wood, he could follow the three-mile circuit, back to the road. There were deep hollows in the river-bank, shoaled with pebbles, as he remembered, perfect places to defend himself from if the horse followed him out there.

The hawthorns that choked the bottom of the wood— some of them good-sized trees—knitted into an almost impassable barrier. He had found a place where the growth thinned slightly and had begun to lift aside the long spiny stems, pushing himself forward, when he stopped. Through the bluish veil of bare twigs he saw the familiar shape out in the field below the wood.

But it seemed not to have noticed him yet. It was looking out across the field towards the river. Quietly, he released himself from the thorns and climbed back across the clearing towards the one side of the wood he had not yet tried. If the horse would only stay down there he could follow his first and easiest plan, up the wood and over the hilltop to the farm.

Now he noticed that the sky had grown much darker. The rain was heavier every second, pressing down as if the earth had to be flooded before nightfall. The oaks ahead blurred and the ground drummed. He began to run. And as he ran he heard a deeper sound running with him. He whirled around. The horse was in the middle of the clearing. It might have been running to get out of the terrific rain except that it was coming straight for him, scattering clay and stones, with an immensely supple and powerful motion. He let out a tearing roar and threw the stone in his right hand. The result was instantaneous. Whether at the roar or the stone the horse reared as if against a wall and shied to the left. As it dropped back on its fore-feet he flung his second stone, at ten yards' range, and saw a bright mud blotch suddenly appear on the glistening black flank. The horse surged down the wood, splashing the earth like water, tossing its long tail as it plunged out of sight among the hawthorns.

He looked around for stones. The encounter had set the blood beating in his head and given him a savage energy. He could have killed the horse at that moment. That this brute should pick him and play with him in this malevolent fashion was more than he could bear. Whoever owned it, he thought, deserved to have its neck broken for letting the dangerous thing loose.

He came out at the woodside, in open battle now, still searching for the right stones. There were plenty here, piled and scattered where they had been ploughed out of the field. He selected two, then straightened and saw the horse twenty yards off in the middle of the steep field, watching him calmly. They looked at each other.

'Out of it!' he shouted, brandishing his arm. 'Out of it! Go on!' The horse twitched its pricked ears. With all his force he threw. The stone soared and landed beyond with a soft thud. He re-armed and threw again. For several minutes he kept up his bombardment without a single hit, working himself into a despair and throwing more and more wildly, till his arm began to ache with the unaccustomed exercise. Throughout the performance the horse watched him fixedly. Finally he had to stop and ease his shoulder muscle. As if the horse had been waiting for just this, it dipped its head twice and came at him.

He snatched up two stones and roaring with all his strength flung the one in his right hand. He was astonished at the crack of the impact. It was as if he had struck a tile—and the horse actually stumbled. With another roar he jumped forward and hurled his other stone. His aim seemed to be under superior guidance. The stone struck and rebounded straight up into the air, spinning fiercely, as the horse swirled away and went careering down towards the far bottom of the field, at first with great, swinging leaps, then at a canter, leaving deep churned holes in the soil.

It turned up the far side of the field, climbing till it was level with him. He felt a little surprise of pity to see it shaking its head, and once it paused to lower its head and paw over its ear with its fore-hoof as a cat does.

'You stay there!' he shouted. 'Keep your distance and you'll not get hurt.'

And indeed the horse did stop at that moment, almost obediently. It watched him as he climbed to the crest.

The rain swept into his face and he realized that he was freezing, as if his very flesh were sodden. The farm seemed miles away over the dreary fields. Without another glance at the horse—he felt too exhausted to care now what it did—he loaded the crook of his left arm with stones and plunged out on to the waste of mud.

He was half-way to the first hedge before the horse appeared, silhouetted against the sky at the corner of the wood, head high and attentive, watching his laborious retreat over the three fields.

The ankle-deep clay dragged at him. Every stride was a separate, deliberate effort, forcing him up and out of the sucking earth, burdened as he was by his sogged clothes and load of stone and limbs that seemed themselves to be turning to mud. He fought to keep his breathing even, two strides in, two strides out, the air ripping his lungs. In the middle of the last field he stopped and looked around. The horse, tiny on the skyline, had not moved.

At the corner of the field he unlocked his clasped arms and dumped the stones by the gatepost, then leaned on the gate. The farm was in front of him. He became conscious of the rain again and suddenly longed to stretch out full-length under it, to take the cooling, healing drops all over his body and forget himself in the last wretchedness of the mud. Making an effort, he heaved his weight over the gate-top. He leaned again, looking up at the hill.

Rain was dissolving land and sky together like a wet water-colour as the afternoon darkened. He concentrated raising his head, searching the skyline from end to end. The horse had vanished. The hill looked lifeless and desolate, an island lifting out of the sea, awash with every tide.

Under the long shed where the tractors, plough, binders and the rest were drawn up, waiting for their seasons, he sat on a sack thrown over a petrol drum, trembling, his lungs heaving. The mingled smell of paraffin, creosote, fertilizer, dust—all was exactly as he had left it twelve years ago. The ragged swallows' nests were still there tucked in the angles of the rafters. He remembered three dead foxes hanging in a row from one of the beams, their teeth bloody.

The ordeal with the horse had already sunk from reality. It hung under the surface of his mind, an obscure confusion of fright and shame, as after a narrowly-escaped street accident. There was a solid pain in his chest, like a spike of bone stabbing, that made him wonder if he had strained his heart on that last stupid burdened run. Piece by piece he began to take off his clothes, wringing the grey water out of them, but soon he stopped that and just sat staring at the ground, as if some important part had been cut out of his brain.

Sunday

Michael marched off to chapel beside his sister, rapping his Sunday shoes down on to the pavement to fetch the brisk, stinging echo off housewalls, wearing the detestable blue blazer with its meaningless badge as a uniform loaded with honours and privilege. In chapel he sat erect, arms folded, instead of curling down on to his spine like a prawn and sinking his chin between his collar-bones as under the steady pressure of a great hand, which was his usual attitude of worship. He sang the hymns and during the prayers thought exultantly of Top Wharf Pub, trying to remember what time those places opened.

All this zest, however, was no match for the sermon. The minister's voice soared among the beams, tireless, as if he were still rehearsing, and after ten minutes these organ-like modulations began to work Michael into a torment of impatience. The nerve-ends all over his body prickled and swarmed. He almost had to sink to his knees. Thoughts of shouting, 'Oh, well!'—one enormous sigh, or simply running out of chapel, brought a fine sweat on to his temples. Finally he closed his eyes and began to imagine a wolf galloping through snow-filled, moonlit forest. Without fail this image was the first thing in his mind whenever he shut his eyes on these situations of constraint, in school, in waiting-rooms, with visitors. The wolf urged itself with all its strength through a land empty of everything but trees and snow. After a while he drifted to vaguer things, a few moments of freedom before his impatience jerked him back to see how the sermon was doing. It was still soaring. He closed his eyes and the wolf was there again.

By the time the doors opened, letting light stream in, he felt stupefied. He edged out with the crowd. Then the eleven-o'clock Sunday sky struck him. He had forgotten it was so early in the day. But with the light and the outside world his mind returned in a rush. Leaving his sister deep in the chapel, buried in a pink and blue bouquet of her friends, and evading the minister who, having processed his congregation generally within, had darted round the side of the chapel to the porch and was now setting his personal seal, a crushing smile and a soft, supporting handclasp, on each member of the flock as they stumbled out, Michael took the three broad steps at a leap and dodged down the crowded path among the graves, like a person with an important dispatch.

But he was no sooner out through the gate than the stitches of his shoes seemed suddenly to tighten, and his damped hair tightened on his scalp. He slowed to a walk.

To the farthest skyline it was Sunday. The valley walls, throughout the week wet, hanging, uncomfortable woods and mud-hole farms, were today neat, remote, and irre-proachably pretty, postcard pretty. The blue sky, the spark-lingly smokeless Sunday air, had disinfected them. Picnickers and chapel-hikers were already up there, sprinkled like con-fetti along the steep lanes and paths, creeping imperceptibly upward towards the brown line of the moors. Spotless, harmless, church-going slopes! Life, over the whole country-side, was suspended for the day.

Below him the town glittered in the clear air and sunlight. Throughout the week it resembled from this point a volcanic pit, bottomless in places, a jagged fissure into a sulphurous underworld, the smoke dragging off the chimneys of the mills and houserows like a tearing fleece. Now it lay as under shallow, slightly warm, clear water, with still streets and bright yards.

There was even something Sundayish about the pavements, something untouchably proper, though nothing had gone over them since grubby Saturday except more feet and darkness.

Superior to all this for once, and quite enjoying it again now he was on his way, Michael went down the hill into the town with strides that jammed his toes into the ends of his shoes. He turned into the Memorial Gardens, past prams, rockeries, forbidden grass, trees with labels, and over the ornamental canal bridge to the bowling greens that lay on the level between canal and river.

His father was there, on the farthest green, with two familiar figures—Harry Rutley, the pork butcher, and Mr Stinson, a tall, sooty, lean man who held his head as if he were blind and spoke rarely, and then only as if phrasing his most private thoughts to himself. A man Michael preferred not to look at. Michael sat on a park bench behind their jack and tried to make himself obvious.

The paths were full of people. Last night this had been a parade of couples, foursomes, gangs and lonely ones—the electricity gathered off looms, sewing-machines and shop counters since Monday milling round the circuit and discharging up the sidepaths among the shrubbery in giggling darkness and shrieks. But now it was families, an after-chapel procession of rustlings and murmurings, lacy bosoms, tight blue pinstripe suits and daisy-chains of children. Soon Michael was worn out, willing the bowls against their bias or against the crown of the green or to roll one foot farther and into the trough or to collide and fall in halves. He could see the Wesleyan Church clock at quarter past eleven and stared at it for what seemed like five minutes, convinced it had stopped.

He stood up as the three men came over to study the pattern of the bowls.

'Are we going now, Dad?'

'Just a minute, lad. Come and have a game.'

That meant at least another game whether he played or not. Another quarter of an hour! And to go and get out a pair of bowls was as good as agreeing to stay there playing till one.

'We might miss him.'

His father laughed. Only just remembering his promise, thought Michael.

'He'll not be there till well on. We shan't miss him.'

His father kicked his bowls together and Harry Rutley slewed the rubber mat into position.

'But will he be there sure?'

Sunday dinner was closer every minute. Then it was sleepy Sunday afternoon. Then Aunt-infested Sunday tea. His father laughed again.

'Billy Red'll be coming down today, won't he, Harry?'

Harry Rutley, pale, slow, round, weighed his jack. He had lost the tip of an ear at the Dardanelles and carried a fragment of his fifth rib on the end of his watch-chain. Now he narrowed his eyes, choosing a particular blade of grass on the far corner of the green.

'Billy Red? Every Sunday. Twelve on the dot.' He dipped his body to the underswing of his arm and came upright as the jack curled away across the green. 'I don't know how he does it.'

The jack had come to rest two feet from the far corner. There followed four more games. They played back to Michael, then across to the far right, then a short one down to the far left, then back to the near right. At last the green was too full, with nine or ten games interweaving and shouts of 'feet' every other minute and bowls bocking together in mid-green.

At quarter to twelve on the clock—Michael now sullen with the punishment he had undergone and the certainty that his day had been played away—the three men came off the

59

CAMROSE LUTHERAN COLLEGE
LIBRARY

green, put away their bowls, and turned down on to the canal bank towpath.

The valley became narrower and its sides steeper. Road, river and canal made their way as best they could, with only a twenty-yard strip of wasteland—a tangle of rank weeds, elderberry bushes and rubble, bleached debris of floods— separating river and canal. Along the far side of the river squeezed the road, rumbling from Monday to Saturday with swaying lorry-loads of cotton and wool and cloth. The valley wall on that side, draped with a network of stone-walled fields and precariously-clinging farms and woods, came down sheer out of the sky into the backyards of a crouched stone row of weavers' cottages whose front doorsteps were almost part of the road. The river ran noisily over pebbles. On the strip of land between river and canal stood Top Wharf Pub— its buildings tucked in under the bank of the canal so that the towpath ran level with the back bedroom windows. On this side the valley wall, with overshadowing woods, dived straight into the black, motionless canal as if it must be a mile deep. The water was quite shallow, however, with its col- lapsed banks and accumulation of mud, so shallow that in some places the rushes grew right across. For years it had brought nothing to Top Wharf Pub but a black greasy damp and rats.

They turned down off the towpath into the wide, cobbled yard in front of the pub.

'You sit here. Now what would you like to drink?'

Michael sat on the cracked, weather-scrubbed bench in the yard under the bar-room window and asked for ginger beer.

'And see if he's come yet. And see if they have any rats ready.'

He had begun to notice the heat and now leaned back against the wall to get the last slice of shade under the eaves. But in no time the sun had moved out over the yard. The valley sides funnelled its rays down as into a trap, dazzling the quartz-points of the worn cobbles, burning the colour off everything. The flies were going wild, swirling in the air, darting and basking on the cobbles—big, green-glossed blue-bottles that leapt on to his hand when he laid it along the hot bench.

In twos and threes men came over the hog-backed bridge leading from the road into the yard, or down off the towpath. Correct, leisurely and a little dazed from morning service, or in overalls that were torn and whitened from obscure Sabbath labours, all disappeared through the door. The hubbub inside thickened. Michael strained to catch some mention of Billy Red.

At last his father brought him his ginger beer and informed him that Billy Red had not arrived yet but everybody was expecting him and he shouldn't be long. They had some nice rats ready.

In spite of the heat, Michael suddenly did not feel like drinking. His whole body seemed to have become frailer and slightly faint, as with hunger. When he sipped, the liquid trickled with a cold, tasteless weight into his disinterested stomach.

He left the glass on the bench and went to the Gents. Afterwards he walked stealthily round the yard, looking in at the old stables and coach-house, the stony cave silences. Dust, cobwebs, rat droppings. Old timbers, old wheels, old harness. Barrels, and rusty stoves. He listened for rats. Walking back across the blinding, humming yard he smelt roast beef and heard the clattering of the pub kitchen and saw through the open window fat arms working over a stove. The whole world was at routine Sunday dinner. The potatoes were already steaming, people sitting about killing time and getting impatient and wishing that something would fall out of the blue and knowing that nothing would. The idea stifled him, he didn't want to think of it. He went quickly back to the bench and sat down, his heart beating as if he had run.

A car nosed over the little bridge and stopped at the far side of the yard, evidently not sure whether it was permitted to enter the yard at all. Out of it stepped a well-to-do young man and a young woman. The young man unbuttoned his pale tweed jacket, thrust his hands into his trouser pockets and came sauntering towards the pub door, the girl on her high heels following beside him, patting her hair and looking round at the scenery as if she had just come up out of a dark pit. They stood at the door for a moment, improvising their final decisions about what she would drink, whether this was the right place, and whether she ought to come in. He was sure it was the right place, this was where they did it all right, and he motioned her to sit on the end of the bench beside Michael. Michael moved accommodatingly to the other end. She ignored him, however, and perched on the last ten inches of the bench, arrayed her wide-skirted, summery, blue-flowered frock over her knees, and busied herself with her mirror. The flies whirled around, inspecting this new thing of scents.

Suddenly there came a shout from the doorway of the pub, long drawn words: 'Here comes the man.'

Immediately several crowded to the doorway, glasses in their hands.

'Here he comes.'

'The Red Killer!'

'Poor little beggar. He looks as if he lives on rat meat.'

'Draw him a half, Gab.'

Over the bridge and into the yard shambled a five-foot, ragged figure. Scarecrowish, tawny to colourless, exhausted, this was Billy Red, the rat-catcher. As a sideline he kept hens, and he had something of the raw, flea-bitten look of a red hen, with his small, sunken features and gingery hair. From the look of his clothes you would think he slept on the hen-house floor, under the roosts. One hand in his pocket, his back at a half-bend, he drifted aimlessly to a stop. Then, to show that after all he had only come for a sit in the sun, he sat down beside Michael with a long sigh.

'It's a grand day,' he announced. His voice was not strong —lungless, a shaky wisp, full of hen-fluff and dust.

Michael peered closely and secretly at this wrinkled, neglected fifty-year-old face shrunk on its small skull. Among the four-day stubble and enlarged pores and deep folds it was hard to make out anything, but there were one or two marks that might have been old rat bites. He had a little withered mouth and kept moving the lips about as if he couldn't get them comfortable. After a sigh he would pause a minute, leaning forward, one elbow on his knees, then sigh again, changing his position, the other elbow now on the other knee, like a man too weary to rest.

'Here you are, Billy.'

A hand held a half-pint high at the pub door like a sign and with startling readiness Billy leapt to his feet and disappeared into the pub, gathering the half-pint on the way and saying:

'I've done a daft bloody thing. I've come down all this way wi'out brass.'

There was an obliging roar of laughter and Michael found himself looking at the girl's powdered profile. She was staring down at her neatly-covered toe as it twisted this way and that, presenting all its polished surfaces.

Things began to sound livelier inside—sharp, loud remarks kicking up bursts of laughter and showering exclamations. The young man came out, composed, serious, and handed the girl a long-stemmed clear glass with a cherry in it. He sat down between her and Michael, splaying his knees as he did so and lunging his face forward to meet his streamingly raised pint—one smooth, expert motion.

'He's in there now,' he said, wiping his mouth. 'They're getting him ready.'

The girl gazed into his face, tilting her glass till the cherry bobbed against her pursed red lips, opening her eyes wide.

Michael looked past her to the doorway. A new figure had appeared. He supposed this must be the landlord, Gab—an aproned hemisphere and round, red greasy face that screwed itself up to survey the opposite hillside.

'Right,' called the landlord. 'I'll get 'em.' Away he went, wiping his hands on his apron, then letting them swing wide of his girth like penguin flippers, towards the coach-house. Now everybody came out of the pub and Michael stood up, surprised to see how many had been crowded in there. They were shouting and laughing, pausing to browse their pints, circulating into scattered groups. Michael went over and stood beside his father who was one of an agitated four. He had to ask twice before he could make himself heard. Even to himself his voice sounded thinner than usual, empty, as if at bottom it wanted nothing so much as to dive into his stomach and hide there in absolute silence, letting events go their own way.

'How many is he going to do?'

'I think they've got two.' His father half turned down towards him. 'It"s usually two or three.'

Nobody took any notice of Billy Red who was standing a little apart, his hands hanging down from the slight stoop that seemed more or less permanent with him, smiling absently at the noisy, hearty groups. He brightened and straightened as the last man out of the pub came across, balancing a brimming pint glass. Michael watched. The moment the pint touched those shrivelled lips the pale little eye set with a sudden strangled intentness. His long, skinny, unshaven throat writhed and the beer shrank away in the glass. In two or three seconds he lowered the glass empty, wiped his mouth on his sleeve and looked around. Then as nobody stepped forward to offer him a fill-up he set the glass down to the cobbles and stood drying his hands on his jacket.

Michael's gaze shifted slightly, and he saw the girl. He recognized his own thoughts in her look of mesmerized incredulity. At her side the young man was watching too, but shrewdly, between steady drinks.

The sun seemed to have come to a stop directly above. Two or three men had taken their jackets off, with irrelevant, noisy clowning, a few sparring feints. Somebody suggested they all go and stand in the canal and Billy Red do his piece under water, and another laughed so hard at this that the beer came spurting from his nostrils. High up on the opposite slope Michael could see a line of Sunday walkers, moving slowly across the dazed grey of the fields. Their coats would be over their shoulders, their ties in their pockets, their shoes agony, the girls asking to be pushed—but if they stood quite still they would feel a breeze. In the cobbled yard the heat had begun to dance.

'Here we are.'

The landlord waddled into the middle of the yard holding up an oblong wire cage. He set it down with a clash on the cobbles.

'Two of the best.'

Everybody crowded round. Michael squeezed to the front and crouched down beside the cage. There was a pause of admiration. Hunched in opposite corners of the cage, their heads low and drawn in and their backs pressed to the wires so that the glossy black-tipped hairs bristled out, were two big brown rats. They sat quiet. A long pinkish-grey tail, thick at the root as his thumb, coiled out by Michael's foot. He touched the hairy tip of it gently with his forefinger.

'Watch out, lad!'

The rat snatched its tail in, leapt across the cage with a crash and gripping one of the zinc bars behind its curved yellow teeth, shook till the cage rattled. The other rat left its corner and began gliding to and fro along one side—a continuous low fluidity, sniffing up and down the bars. Then both rats stopped and sat up on their hind-legs, like persons coming out of a trance, suddenly recognizing people. Their noses quivered as they directed their set, grey-chinned, inquisitive expressions at one face after another.

The landlord had been loosening the nooses in the end of two long pieces of dirty string. He lifted the cage again.

'Catch a tail, Walt.'

The group pressed closer. A hand came out and roamed in readiness under the high-held cage floor. The rats moved uneasily. The landlord gave the cage a shake and the rats crashed. A long tail swung down between the wires. The hand grabbed and pulled.

'Hold it.'

The landlord slipped the noose over the tail, down to the very butt, and pulled it tight. The caught rat, not quite convinced before but now understanding the whole situation, doubled round like a thing without bones, and bit and shook the bars and forced its nose out between them to get at the string that held its buttocks tight to the cage side.

'Just you hold that string, Walt. So's it can't get away when we open up.'

Now the landlord lifted the cage again, while Walt held his string tight. The other rat, watching the operation on its companion, had bunched up in a corner, sitting on its tail.

'Clever little beggar. You know what I'm after, don't you?'

The landlord gave the cage a shake, but the rat clung on, its pink feet gripping the wires of the cage floor like hands. He shook the cage violently.

'Move, you stubborn little beggar,' demanded the landlord. He went on shaking the cage with sharp, jerking movements.

Then the rat startled everybody. Squeezing still farther into its corner, it opened its mouth wide and began to scream— a harsh, ripping, wavering scream travelling out over the

66

yard like some thin, metallic, dazzling substance that decomposed instantly. As one scream died the rat started another, its mouth wide. Michael had never thought a rat could make so much noise. As it went on at full intensity, his stomach began to twist and flex like a thick muscle. For a moment he was so worried by these sensations that he stopped looking at the rat. The landlord kept on shaking the cage and the scream shook in the air, but the rat clung on, still sitting on its tail.

'Give him a poke, Gab, stubborn little beggar!'

The landlord held the cage still, reached into his top pocket and produced a pencil. At this moment, Michael saw the girl, extricating herself from the press, pushing out backwards. The ring of rapt faces and still legs closed again. The rat was hurtling round the cage, still screaming, leaping over the other, attacking the wires first at this side then at that. All at once it crouched in a corner, silent. A hand came out and grabbed the loop of tail. The other noose was there ready. The landlord set the cage down.

Now the circle relaxed and everyone looked down at the two rats flattened on the cage bottom, their tails waving foolishly outside the wires.

'Well then, Billy,' said the landlord. 'How are they?'

Billy Red nodded and grinned.

'Them's grand,' he said. 'Grand.' His little rustling voice made Michael want to cough.

'Right. Stand back.'

Everybody backed obediently, leaving the cage, Walt with his foot on one taut string and the landlord with his foot on the other in the middle of an arena six or seven yards across. Michael saw the young man on the far side, his glass still half full in his hand. The girl was nowhere to be seen.

Billy Red peeled his coat off, exposing an old shirt, army issue, most of the left arm missing. He pulled his trousers up under his belt, spat on his hands, and took up a position which placed the cage door a couple of paces or so from his left side and slightly in front of him. He bent forward a little more than usual, his arms hanging like a wary wrestler's, his eye fixed on the cage.

'Eye like a bloody sparrow-hawk,' somebody murmured.

There was a silence. The landlord waited, kneeling now beside the cage. Nothing disturbed the dramatic moment but the distant, brainless church bells.

'This one first, Walt,' said the landlord. 'Ready, Billy?'

He pushed down the lever that raised the cage door and let his rat have its full five- or six-yard length of string. He had the end looped round his hand. Walt kept his rat on a tight string.

Everybody watched intently. The freed rat pulled its tail in delicately and sniffed at the noose round it, ignoring the wide-open door. Then the landlord reached to tap the cage and in a flash the rat vanished.

Michael lost sight of it. But he saw Billy Red spin half round and drop smack down on his hands and knees on the cobbles.

'He's got it!'

Billy Red's face was compressed in a snarl and as he snapped his head from side to side the dark, elongated body of the rat whipped around his neck. He had it by the shoulders. Michael's eyes fixed like cameras.

A dozen shakes, and Billy Red stopped, his head lowered. The rat hanging from his mouth was bunching and relaxing, bunching and relaxing. He waited. Everyone waited. Then the rat spasmed, fighting with all its paws, and Billy shook again wildly, the rat's tail flying like a lash. This time when he stopped the body hung down limply. The piece of string, still attached to the tail, trailed away across the cobbles.

Gently Billy took the rat from his mouth and laid it down. He stood up, spat a couple of times, and began to wipe his mouth, smiling shamefacedly. Everybody breathed out—an exclamation of marvelling disgust and admiration, and loud above the rest:

'Pint now, Billy?'

The landlord walked back into the pub and most of the audience followed him to refresh their glasses. Billy Red stood separate, still wiping his mouth with a scrap of snuff-coloured cloth.

Michael went over and bent to look at the dead rat. Its shoulders were wet-black with saliva, and the fur bitten. It lay on its left side, slightly curved, its feet folded, its eyes still round and bright in their alert, inquisitive expression. He touched its long, springy whiskers. A little drip of blood was puddling under its nose on the cobblestones. As he watched, a bluebottle alighted on its tail and sprang off again, then suddenly reappeared on its nose, inspecting the blood.

He walked over to the cage. Walt was standing there talking, his foot on the taut string. This rat crouched against the wires as if they afforded some protection. It made no sign of noticing Michael as he bent low over it. Its black beads stared outward fixedly, its hot brown flanks going in and out. There was a sparkle on its fur, and as he looked more closely, thinking it must be perspiration, he became aware of the heat again.

He stood up, a dull pain in his head. He put his hand to his scalp and pressed the scorch down into his skull, but that didn't seem to connect with the dull, thick pain.

'I'm off now, Dad,' he called.

'Already? Aren't you going to see this other one?'

'I think I'll go.' He set off across the yard.

'Finish your drink,' his father called after him.

He saw his glass almost full on the end of the white bench but walked past it and round the end of the pub and up on to the tow-path. The sycamore trees across the canal arched over black damp shade and the still water. High up, the valley slopes were silvered now, frizzled with the noon brightness. The earthen tow-path was like stone. Fifty yards along he passed the girl in the blue-flowered frock sauntering back towards the pub, pulling at the heads of the tall bank grasses.

'Have they finished yet?' she asked.

Michael shook his head. He found himself unable to speak. With all his strength he began to run.

Snow

And let me repeat this over and over again: beneath my feet
is the earth, some part of the surface of the earth. Beneath the
snow, beneath my feet, that is. What else could it be? It is
firm, I presume, and level. If it is not actually soil and rock,
it must be ice. It is very probably ice. Whichever it may be, it
is proof—the most substantial proof possible—that I am
somewhere on the earth, the known earth. It would be
absurd to dig down through the snow, just to determine
exactly what is underneath, earth or ice. This bedded snow
may well be dozens of feet deep. Besides, the snow filling
all the air and rivering along the ground would pour into
the hole as fast as I could dig, and cover me too—very
quickly.

This could be no other planet: the air is perfectly natural,
perfectly good.

Our aircraft was forced down by this unusual storm. The
pilot tried to make a landing, but misjudged the extra-
ordinary power of the wind and the whereabouts of the
ground. The crash was violent. The fuselage buckled and
gaped, and I was flung clear. Unconscious of everything save
the need to get away from the disaster, I walked farther off
into the blizzard and collapsed, which explains why when I
came to full consciousness and stood up out of the snow that
was burying me I could see nothing of either the aircraft or
my fellow passengers. All around me was what I have been
looking at ever since. The bottomless dense motion of snow.
I started to walk.

Of course, everything previous to that first waking may have been entirely different since I don't remember a thing about it. Whatever chance dropped me here in the snow evidently destroyed my memory. That's one thing of which there is no doubt whatsoever. It is, so to speak, one of my facts. The aircraft crash is a working hypothesis, that merely.

There's no reason why I should not last quite a long time yet. I seem to have an uncommon reserve of energy. To keep my mind firm, that is the essential thing, to fix it firmly in my reasonable hopes, and lull it there, encourage it. Mesmerize it slightly with a sort of continuous prayer. Because when my mind is firm, my energy is firm. And that's the main thing here—energy. No matter how circumspect I may be, or how lucid, without energy I am lost on the spot. Useless to think about it. Where my energy ends I end, and all circumspection and all lucidity end with me. As long as I have energy I can correct my mistakes, outlast them, outwalk them—for instance the unimaginable error that as far as I know I am making at this very moment. This step, this, the next five hundred, or five thousand—all mistaken, all absolute waste, back to where I was ten hours ago. But we recognize that thought. My mind is not my friend. My support, my defence, but my enemy too—not perfectly intent on getting me out of this. If I were mindless perhaps there would be no difficulty whatsoever. I would simply go on aware of nothing but my step by step success in getting over the ground. The thing to do is to keep alert, keep my mind fixed in alertness, recognize these treacherous paralysing, yes, lethal thoughts the second they enter, catch them before they can make that burrowing plunge down the spinal cord.

Then gently and without any other acknowledgment push them back—out into the snow where they belong. And that *is* where they belong. They are infiltrations of the snow, encroachments of this immensity of lifelessness. But they enter so slyly! We are true, they say, or at least very probably true, and on that account you must entertain us and even give us the run of your life, since above all things you are dedicated to the truth. That is the air they have, that's how they come in. What do I know about the truth? As if simple-minded dedication to truth were the final law of existence! I only know more and more clearly what is good for me. It's my mind that has this contemptible awe for the probably true, and my mind, I know, I prove it every minute, is not me and is by no means sworn to help me. Am I to lie? I must survive —that's a truth sacred as any, and as the hungry truths devour the sleepy truths I shall digest every other possible truth to the substance and health and energy of my own, and the ones I can't digest I shall spit out, since in this situation my intention to survive is the one mouth, the one digestive tract, so to speak, by which I live. But those others! I relax for a moment, I leave my mind to itself for a moment—and they are in complete possession. They plunge into me, exultantly, mercilessly. There is no question of their intention or their power. Five seconds of carelessness, and they have struck. The strength melts from me, my bowels turn to water, my consciousness darkens and shrinks, I have to stop.

What are my facts? I do have some definite facts.

Taking six steps every five seconds, I calculate—allowing for my brief regular sleeps—that I have been walking through this blizzard for five months and during that time have covered something equal to the breadth of the Atlantic between Southampton and New York. Two facts. And a third: throughout those five months this twilight of snow has not grown either darker or brighter.

So.

There seems no reason to doubt that I am somewhere within either the Arctic or the Antarctic Circle. That's a comfort. it means my chances of survival are not uniquely bad. Men have walked the length of Asia simply to amuse themselves.

73

Obviously I am not travelling in a straight line. But that needn't give me any anxiety. Perhaps I made a mistake when I first started walking, setting my face against the wind instead of downwind. Coming against the wind I waste precious energy and there is always this wearisome snow blocking my eyes and mouth. But I had to trust the wind. This resignation to the wind's guidance is the very foundation of my firmness of mind. The wind is not simply my compass. In fact, I must not think of it as a compass at all. The wind is my law. As a compass nothing could be more useless. No need to dwell on that. It's extremely probable indeed and something I need not hide from myself that this wind is leading me to and fro in quite a tight little maze—always shifting too stealthily for me to notice the change. Or, if the sun is circling the horizon, it seems likely that the wind is swinging with it through the three hundred and sixty degrees once in every twenty-four hours, turning me as I keep my face against it in a perfect circle not more than seven miles across. This would explain the otherwise strange fact that in spite of the vast distance I have covered the terrain is still dead level, exactly as when I started. A frozen lake, no doubt. This is a strong possibility and I must get used to it without letting it overwhelm me, and without losing sight of its real advantages.

The temptation to trust to luck and instinct and cut out across wind is to be restricted. The effect on my system of confidence would be disastrous. My own judgment would naturally lead me in a circle. I would have to make deliberate changes of direction to break out of that circle—only to go in a larger circle or a circle in the opposite direction. So more changes. Wilder and more sudden changes, changes of my changes—all to evade an enemy that showed so little sign of itself it might as well not have existed. It's clear where all that would end. Shouting and running and so on. Staggering round like a man beset by a mob. Falling, grovelling. So on. The snow.

No. All I have to do is endure: that is, keep my face to the wind. My face to the wind, a firm grip on my mind, and everything else follows naturally. There is not the slightest need to be anxious. Any time now the Polar night will arrive, bringing a drastic change of climate—inevitable. Clearing the sky and revealing the faultless compass of the stars.

The facts are overwhelmingly on my side. I could almost believe in Providence. After all, if one single circumstance were slightly—only slightly—other than it is! If, for instance, instead of waking in a blizzard on a firm level place I had come to consciousness falling endlessly through snow-cloud. Then I might have wondered very seriously whether I were in the gulf or not. Or if the atmosphere happened to consist of, say, ammonia. I could not have existed. And in the moment before death by asphyxiation I would certainly have been convinced I was out on some lifeless planet. Or if I had no body but simply arms and legs growing out of a head, my whole system of confidence would have been disoriented from the start. My dreams, for instance, would have been meaningless to me, or rather an argument of my own mean-inglessness. I would have died almost immediately, out of sheer bewilderment. It wouldn't need nearly such extreme differences either. If I had been without those excellent pig-skin boots, trousers, jacket, gloves and hood, the cold would have extinguished me at once.

And even if I had double the clothing that I have, where would I be without my chair? My chair is quite as important as one of my lungs. As both my lungs, indeed, for without it I should be dead. Where would I have slept? Lying in the snow. But lying flat, as I have discovered, I am buried by the snow in just under a minute, and the cold begins to take over my hands and my feet and my face. Sleep would be impossible. In other words, I would very soon collapse of exhaustion and be buried. As it is, I unsnap my chair harness, plant the chair in the snow, sit on it, set my feet on the rung between the front legs, my arms folded over my knees and my head resting on my arms, and am able in this way to take a sleep of fully ten minutes before the snow piles over me.

The chain of providential coincidences is endless. Or rather, like a chain mail, it is complete without one missing link to betray and annul the rest. Even my dreams are part of it. They are as tough and essential a link as any, since there can no longer be any doubt that they are an accurate reproduction of my whole previous life, of the world as it is and as I knew it—all without one contradictory detail. Yet if my amnesia had been only a little bit stronger!—it needed only that. Because without this evidence of the world and my identity I could have known no purpose in continuing the ordeal. I could only have looked, breathed and died, like a nestling fallen from the nest.

Everything fits together. And the result—my survival, and my determination to survive. I should rejoice.

The chair is of conventional type: nothing in the least mystifying about it. A farmhouse sort of chair: perfectly of a piece with my dreams, as indeed are my clothes, my body and all the inclinations of my mind. It is of wood, painted black, though in places showing a coat of brown beneath the black. One of the nine struts in the back is missing and some child—I suppose it was a child—has stuck a dab of chewing-gum into the empty socket. Obviously the chair has been well used, and not too carefully. The right foreleg has been badly chewed, evidently by a puppy, and on the seat both black and brown paints are wearing through showing the dark grain of the pale wood. If all this is not final evidence of a reality beyond my own, of the reality of the world it comes from, the world I re-dream in my sleeps—I might as well lie down in the snow and be done with.

The curious harness needn't worry me. The world, so far as I've dreamed it at this point, contains no such harness, true.

But since I've not yet dreamed anything from after my twenty-sixth birthday, the harness might well have been invented between that time and the time of my disaster. Probably it's now in general use. Or it may be the paraphernalia of some fashionable game that came in during my twenty-seventh or later year, and to which I got addicted. Sitting on snow peaks in nineteenth-century chairs. Or perhaps I developed a passion for painting polar scenery and along with that a passion for this particular chair as my painting seat, and had the harness designed specially. A lucky eccentricity! It is perfectly adapted to my present need. But all that's in the dark still. There's a lot I haven't dreamed yet. From my twenty-third and twenty-fourth years I have almost nothing—a few insignificant episodes. Nothing at all after my twenty-sixth birthday. The rest, though, is about complete, which suggests that any time now I ought to be getting my twenty-third and twenty-fourth years in full and, more important, my twenty-seventh year, or as much of it as there is, along with the accurate account of my disaster and the origin of my chair.

There seems little doubt of my age. Had I been dreaming my life chronologically there would have been real cause for worry. I could have had no idea how much was still to come. Of course, if I were suddenly to dream something from the middle of my sixtieth year I would have to reorganize all my ideas. What really convinces me of my youth is my energy. The appearance of my body tells me nothing. Indeed, from my hands and feet—which are all I have dared to uncover— one could believe I was several hundred years old, or even dead, they are so black and shrunken on the bone. But the emaciation is understandable, considering that for five months I have been living exclusively on will-power, without the slightest desire for food.

I have my job to get back to, and my mother and father will be in despair. And God knows what will have happened to

Helen. Did I marry her? I have no wedding ring. But we were engaged. And it is another confirmation of my youth that my feelings for her are as they were then—stronger, in fact, yes a good deal stronger, though speaking impartially these feelings that seem to be for her might easily be nothing but my desperate longing to get back to the world in general—a longing that is using my one-time affection for Helen as a sort of form or model. It's possible, very possible, that I have in reality forgotten her, even that I am sixty years old, that she has been dead for thirty-four years. Certain things may be very different from what I imagine. If I were to take this drift of thoughts to the logical extreme there is no absolute proof that my job, my parents, Helen and the whole world are not simply my own invention, fantasies my imagination has improvized on the simple themes of my own form, my clothes, my chair, and the properties of my present environment. I am in no position to be sure about anything.

But there is more to existence, fortunately, than consideration of possibilities. There is conviction, faith. If there were not, where would I be? The moment I allow one of these 'possibilities' the slightest intimacy—a huge futility grips me, as it were physically, by the heart, as if the organ itself were despairing of this life and ready to give up.

Courageous and calm. That should be my prayer. I should repeat that, repeat it like the Buddhists with their 'O jewel of the lotus'. Repeat it till it repeats itself in my very heart, till every heartbeat drives it through my whole body. Courageous and calm. This is the world, think no more about it.

My chair will keep me sane. My chair, my chair, my chair —I might almost repeat that. I know every mark on it, every grain. So near and true! It alone predicates a Universe, the entire Universe, with its tough carpentering, its sprightly, shapely design—so delicate, so strong. And while I have the game I need be afraid of nothing. Though it is dangerous. Tempting, dangerous, but—it is enough to know that the joy is mine. I set the chair down in the snow, letting myself think I am going to sleep, but instead of sitting I step back a few paces into the snow. How did I think of that? The first time, I did not dare look away from it. I had never before let it out of my hand, never let it go for a fraction between unbuckling it and sitting down on it. But then I let it go and stepped back into the snow. I had never heard my voice before. I was astonished at the sound that struggled up out of me. Well, I need the compensations. And this game does rouse my energies, so it is, in a sense, quite practical. After the game, I could run. That's the moment of danger, though, the moment of overpowering impatience when I could easily lose control and break out, follow my instinct, throw myself on luck, run out across the wind.

But there is a worse danger. If I ran out across the wind I would pretty soon come to my senses, turn my face back into the wind. It is the game itself, the stage of development it has reached, that is dangerous now, I no longer simply step back. I set the chair down, turn my face away and walk off into the blizzard, counting my steps carefully. At fourteen paces I stop. Fifteen is the limit of vision in this dense flow of snow, so at fourteen I stop, and turn. Let those be the rules. Let me fix the game at that. Because at first I see nothing. That should be enough for me. Everywhere, pouring silent grey, a silence like a pressure, like the slow coming to bear of some incalculable pressure, too gradual to detect. If I were simply to stand there my mind would crack in a few moments. But I concentrate, I withdraw my awe from the emptiness and look pointedly into it. At first, everything is as usual—as I have seen it for five months. Then my heart begins to thump unnaturally, because I seem to make out a dimness, a shadow that wavers deep in the grey turmoil, vanishes and darkens, rises and falls. I step one pace forward and using all my willpower stop again. The shadow is as it was. Another step. The shadow seems to be a little darker. Then it vanishes and I lunge two steps forward but immediately stop because there it is, quite definite, no longer moving. Slowly I walk towards it. The rules are that I keep myself under control, that I restrain all sobs or shouts though of course it is impossible to keep the breathing regular—at this stage at least, and right up to the point where the shadow resolves into a chair. In that vast grey dissolution—my chair! The snowflakes are drifting against the legs and gliding between the struts, bumping against them, clinging and crawling over the seat. To control myself then is not within human power. Indeed I seem to more or less lose consciousness at that point. I'm certainly not responsible for the weeping, shouting thing that falls on my chair, embracing it, kissing it, bruising his cheeks against it. As the snowflakes tap and run over my gloves and over the chair I begin to call them names. I peer into each one as if it were a living face, full of speechless recognition, and I call to them—Willy, Joanna, Peter, Jesus, Ferdinand, anything that comes into my head, and shout to them and nod and laugh. Well, it's a harmless enough madness.

The temptation to go beyond the fourteen paces is now becoming painful. To go deep into the blizzard. Forty paces. Then come back, peering. Fifteen paces, twenty paces. Stop. A shadow.

That would not be harmless madness. If I were to leave my chair like that the chances are I would never find it again. My footprints do not exist in this undertow of snow. Weeks later, I would still be searching, casting in great circles, straining at every moment to pry a shadow out of the grey sameness. My chair meanwhile a hundred miles away in the blizzard, motionless—neat legs and elegant back, sometimes buried, sometimes uncovering again. And for centuries, long after I'm finished, still sitting there, intact with its toothmarks and missing strut, waiting for a darkening shape to come up out of the nothingness and shout to it and fall on it and possess it.

But my chair is here, on my back, here. There's no danger of my ever losing it. Never so long as I keep control, keep my mind firm. All the facts are on my side. I have nothing to do but endure.

The Harvesting

'And I shall go into a hare
With sorrow and sighs and mickle care'

Mr Grooby kept his eyes down. The tractor and reaper below, negotiating the bottom right corner of the narrow, steep triangle of wheat, bumbled and nagged and stopped and started. The sweat trickled at the corner of his eye. Not a breath of air moved to relieve him. A dull atmosphere of pain had settled just above eyelevel, and he had the impression that the whole top of heaven had begun to glare and flame.

For nearly three hours, since nine that morning, not the faintest gossamer of cloud had intervened between the sun and the thin felt of his trilby. A sunbather would have escaped to cover an hour ago.

Ten more minutes would finish the field. The best sport of all, he knew, usually comes in the last ten minutes. He would be a fool to go off and miss that after waiting for it, earning it, so to speak, all morning.

Laying his gun over a prone sheaf, he stripped off his waistcoat and draped that beside the gun, then raised his trilby and mopped the bald dome under it with his handkerchief, taking a few steps out and back again to bring the air to some coolness against his brow.

This was surely unnatural heat. He could remember nothing like it. The hanging dust raised by the tractor and the hurrying blade of the cutter absorbed the sun's vibrations till it seemed hot as only a solid substance ought to be. And the spluttering reports, and dense machine-gun bursts from the tractor as it started up the gradient, tore holes in the blanket-ing air with something fierier and deadlier. Near the edge of the field the dark, scorched-looking figures of out-of-work or off-work colliers, gathering the sheaves into stooks, with their black or tan whippets bounding around them, and one big, white, bony greyhound, appeared hellish, as if they flitted to and fro in not quite visible flames.

This was Grooby's first day out in the open since the previous summer. He had intended to stay out for only a couple of hours, expecting the field to be finished by eleven. Two hours today, four or five tomorrow, and so on, acclima-tizing himself gradually, till he could take a whole day and enjoy the whole harvest. Perhaps three hours was a bit too much to begin with; perhaps he was overdoing it.

Ten more minutes then, and he would leave. Ten more minutes and after that, no matter how little of the field was left to cut, he would leave. He didn't want to spoil his holiday at the start.

By standing perfectly still, leaving his body to the sun's rays and shrinking inwardly from all its surfaces, he found he could defy both the slowness of time and the huge enveloping weight of the heat. He crouched in a tiny darkness some-where near the bottom of his spine and dreamed of his car in the stone barn half a mile behind him across the fields. He smelt the cool leather of the upholstery and the fresh, thickly-daubed mustard and beef sandwiches lying there with two bottles of beer under the rug on the back seat.

The tractor came up to make its looping turn at the top corner. As Grooby stepped back, the grizzled chimpanzee figure at the wheel shouted something at him and jabbed a finger down toward the wheat, and the long, dark-brown creature perched above the cutter shouted and pointed at the wheat, while the shuddering combination slewed round on itself, suddenly disgorging its roar over Grooby as if a door had opened. Then the blade swept in again, wheat ears raining down under the red paddles of the reaper, every few feet a new sheaf leaping out on to the stubble—so many activities, so much hot busy iron, in a wake of red dust, drawing off, leaving Grooby isolated and surprisingly whole, as if he too had been tossed out like one of the sheafs.

Roused, he stepped up close and resumed his watch down the two diverging walls of stalks. The shouts of the farmer and his man meant they had seen something in the patch. Whatever remained in there would be whisking from side to side like fish trapped in shallowing water as the reaper closed in. Grooby held his gun in the crook of his left arm, like a baby, fondling the chased side-plates and trigger-guard and mentally rehearsing for the hundredth time the easy swing, overtaking the running shape with a smooth squeeze on the trigger and follow through—one gliding, effortless motion, like a gesture in conversation.

Fifty yards behind him, two dead rabbits lay under a sheaf. He had missed three. His shooting was not good. But he loved the occasion—or rather, he had looked forward to it, remembering the days last summer when rabbits had been flying out in all directions, getting themselves snagged in the cutter, or bowled over by the colliers' sticks, or rolled in a flurry of dust by the dogs, and he himself shooting to left and right like a hero at a last stand. That was the sport, banging away.

But last summer there had been no such heat. He wondered if the farmer thought it unusual. Maybe it was a record heat-wave following the freakish dispersal during the night of some protective layer in the upper atmosphere. The Sunday papers would be full of it, with charts and historical comparisons.

Or maybe he was simply growing old, beginning to fail in the trials. He imagined there must be certain little tests that showed the process clearly: a day of rain, the first snow, or, as now, a few hours in the sun. Were these to become terrors? And he had put on a few pounds since last summer.

The trilby was a mistake. His brain felt black and numb and solid, like a hot stone. Tomorrow he would bring a broad-brimmed Panama hat. The stookers would snigger, no doubt, but they knotted handkerchiefs over their heads, like little boys.

He watched the tractor turning again at the bottom of the strip and it was now, as the tractor started up the slope towards him, that a strange sensation came over Grooby. Whether at the idea of all the energy needed and being exerted to drag such a weight of vibrating iron up that hill in that heat, or at the realization that here was help approaching, and he could therefore allow himself to yield a little to the sun, he suddenly lost control of his limbs and felt himself floating in air a few feet above the crushed stubble.

He sat down hastily, adjusting his pose to look as natural as possible, but neverthless alarmed and with a deep conviction that he was too late. He had closed his eyes and heard a voice in the darkness announcing over and over, in brisk, business-like tones, that he would now leave the field immediately. The sun had gathered to a small red spot in the top of his brain. He thought with terror of the distance back to the farm and safety: the short walk seemed to writhe and twist like a filament over a gulf of fire.

Opening his eyes, he found the tractor's Ford headplate, as it climbed towards him, centering his vision, and like a drunken man he anchored his attention to that as if it were the last spark of consciousness. Slowly his head cleared. He changed his position.

And now, as the world reassembled, he became aware that the farmer was standing erect in the tractor, waving his free arm and shouting. Grooby looked round for some explanation. The stookers had stopped work and were looking towards him, straining towards him almost like leashed dogs, while the dogs themselves craned round, quivering with anxiety, tucking their tails in for shame at seeing nothing where they knew there was something, eager to see something and be off. Grooby took all this in remotely, as through the grill of a visor. He had a dim notion that they were all warning him back from the brink of something terrible. Then his eyes focused.

A yard out from the wall of wheat, ten yards from Grooby and directly in the path of the tractor, a large hare sat erect.

It stared fixedly, as if it had noted some suspicious detail in the far distance. Actually it was stupefied by this sudden revelation of surrounding enemies. Driven all morning from one side of the shrinking wheat to the other, terrified and exhausted by the repeated roaring charge and nearer and nearer miss of the tractor in its revolutions, the hare's nerves had finally cracked and here it was in the open, trying to recognize the strangely shorn hillside, confronted by the shapes of men and dogs, with the tractor coming up again to the left and a man scrambling to his feet on the skyline above to the right.

So it sat up, completely nonplussed.

Grooby aimed mercilessly. But then he perceived that the farmer's shouts had redoubled and altered in tone, and the farmhand on the cutter had joined in the shouting, flourishing his arms, with violent pushing movements away to his left, as if Grooby's gun muzzles were advancing on his very chest. Accordingly, Grooby realized that the tractor, too, lay above his gun barrels. He held his aim for a moment, not wanting to forgo his prior claim on the hare, and glanced over towards the dogs, flustered and angry. But for those dogs the hare would surely have run straight out, giving a clean, handsome shot. Now, any moment, the dogs would come clowning across the field, turn the hare back into the wheat and hunt it right through and away out at the bottom into the uncut field of rye down there, or round the back of the hill in to the other fields.

To anticipate the dogs, Grooby started to run to the left, down the other side of the wheat, thinking to bring the hare against open background. But before he had gone three strides, the hare was off, an uncertain, high-eared, lolloping gait, still unable to decide the safe course or the right speed, till the dogs came ripping long smouldering tracks up the field and Grooby fired.

He forgot all about swing and squeeze and follow through. He was enraged, off balance, distracted by the speeding dogs and at all times hated shots from left to right. But his target loomed huge, close, and moving slowly. The gun jarred back on his shoulder. The hare somersaulted, as if tossed into the air by the hind legs, came down in a flash of dust and streaked back into the wheat.

For a second, Grooby thought he must have fainted. He could hear the farmer yelling to the colliers to call their dogs off, threatening to shoot the bloody lot, but the voice came wierdly magnified and distorted as if his hearing had lost its muting defences. His head spun in darkness. He knew he had fallen. He could hear the tractor protesting on the gradient and it seemed so near, the engine drove so cruelly into his ears, he wondered if he had fallen in front of it. The ground trembled beneath him. Surely they would see him lying there. His sense cleared a little and as at the moment of waking from nightmare to the pillow and the familiar room, Grooby realized he was lying face downward in the wheat.

He must have fainted and staggered into the wheat and fallen there. But why hadn't they noticed him? Twisting his head, he saw what he could scarcely believe, the red paddling flails of the reaper coming up over him. Within seconds those terrible hidden ground-shaving blades would melt the stalks and touch him—he would be sawn clean in two. He had seen them slice rabbits like bacon.

He uttered a cry, to whoever might hear, and rolled sideways, dragging himself on his elbows, tearing up the wheat in his hands as he clawed his way out of the path of the mutilator, and cried again, this time in surprise, as a broad wrench of pain seemed to twist off the lower half of his body, so that for a moment he thought the blades had caught him. With a final convulsion he threw himself forward and sprawled parallel to the course of the tractor.

This is how it happens, his brain was yammering: it can happen, it can happen, and it's happened. This is how it happens. Everything is going nicely, then one careless touch, one wink of a distraction, and your whole body's in the mincer, and you're in the middle of it, the worst that can happen forever. You've never dreamed it possible and all your life it's been this fraction of a second away, a hair's breadth from you, and here it is, here it is.

The noise of the tractor and the special grinding clatter of the cutter seemed to come up out of the raw soil, taking possession of all the separate atoms of his body. The tractor's outline rose black against the blue sky and Grooby saw the farmer standing at the wheel, looking down. He cried out and waved an arm, like a drowning man, whereupon the farmer pointed at him, shouting something. Then the flails came over, and he heard the blades wuthering in the air. For a second everything disintegrated in din, chaffy fragments and dust, then they had gone past, and Grooby lay panting. Why hadn't they stopped? They saw him and went straight past. The end of the cutter bar had gone by inches from his face, and now he could see through the thin veil of stalks and out over the naked stubble slope. Why hadn't they stopped and got down to help him? He gathered himself and once more tried to get to his feet, but the baked clods of soil and the bright, metallic stalks of wheat fled into a remote silent picture as the pain swept up his back again and engulfed him.

But only for a moment. He jerked up his head. Hands held his shoulders, and someone splashed his face with water that

ran down his neck and over his chest. He shook himself free
and stood. As if he had tripped only accidentally, he began to
beat the dust from his trousers and elbows, ignoring the ring
of men who had come up and stood in a circle watching. All
the time he was trying to recall exactly what happened. He
remembered, as if touching a forgotten dream, that he had
been lying in the wheat. Had they carried him out then? He
flexed his back cautiously, but that felt easy, with no trace
of discomfort. The farmer handed him his trilby.

'All right now?'

He nodded. 'Gun must have caught me off balance. Only
explanation. Held it too loose. Knocked me clean out.'

He adopted his brusquest managerial air, putting the
farmer and this gang of impudent, anonymous colliers' faces
back into place. What had they seen, he wondered. They
could tell him. But how could he possibly ask?

'One of those flukes,' he added.

The farmer was watching him thoughtfully, as if expecting
him to fall again.

'Well, what happened to the hare?' Grooby demanded.

His continued gusty assurance took effect. Whatever they
had seen or were suspecting, they had to take account of this
voice. The farmer nodded, in his ancient, withered-up way.
'You're all right, then.' He turned on the stookers in sur-
prising fury. '*What the hell am I paying you for?*'

As they all trooped off down the field with their sullen
dogs, the farmer started the tractor up and the cutter blade
blurred into life.

Left alone, Grooby sank into a shocked stupor. His mind
whirled around like a fly that dared not alight. A black
vacancy held him. Something important was going on, if only
he could grasp it. He seemed unable to move, even to wipe
away the sweat that collected in his eyebrows and leaked
down into his eyes. It occurred to him that the sun had
settled over the earth, so that the air was actually burning

gas, depth of flame in every direction. He watched the tractor dwindle in the bottom of the field, as if it were melting into a glittering puddle in the haze. How could men go on working in that temperature? The stookers were clearly charring; they were black as burnt twigs, tiny black ant men moving on the grey field.

One cut up and one down would finish the piece, and this prospect partly revived Grooby, including him once more in events. As the tractor waded up one side—now only fifteen yards or so long—he walked down the other, scrutinizing the thin curtain of stalks where every clump of weeds had ears and seemed to be sitting up alert.

At the bottom, a few paces back into the stubble, Grooby took up his position for the final sweep. Now the hare must either show itself or be killed by the cutter, unless it had already died in there of that first shot. As the tractor bore down, the colliers left their work, edging forward till Grooby noticed they had moved up level with him, as if to supervise the kill. He advanced a little, separating himself. The thought that the hare's first appearance would bring two or three dogs dancing across the line of fire unnerved him. Also, he didn't want these men to be looking at his face, which felt to be ludicrously pink and sweating its very fat.

If only the tractor would hurry up and get it over with or if only the hare would gather its wits and move. But the tractor seemed to have stopped. Grooby blinked and straightened himself vigorously, and that brought the tractor on a little more quickly. From the lowest corner of the wheat the few stalks that would be last to fall leaned out and tormented him in those endless seconds.

Then all at once here was the hare, huge as if nothing else existed. The colliers shouted, and the gun jumped to Grooby's shoulder. But he held his fire. The animal was too near. He saw the roughness of its brindled, gingery flanks and the delicate lines of its thin face. Besides, it seemed to want to surrender, and was so obviously bewildered that for a moment Grooby felt more like shooing it away to safety than shooting it dead. But it had already realized its folly and swerving sharply to Grooby's right, launched itself up the hill like a dart, a foot above the ground, while the farmer stood shouting in the tractor as those last stalks fell and the dogs behind Grooby climbed the air yelling and coughing on their restrained collars.

He had bare seconds, he knew, before the dogs broke loose all around him, and it was with half his attention behind him that Grooby fired, at ten yards' range. The hare flattened in a scatter of dust, but was on its feet again, flogging its way up the slope, more heavily now, its hindquarters collapsing every few strides. It looked just about finished, and rather than spoil it with the choke barrel or miss it clean, and also in order to be ahead of those dogs whatever happened, Grooby set off at a lumbering run. Immediately the hare picked up and stretched away ahead. Grooby stopped and aimed. The sweat flooded his eyes and he felt he ought to sit. He heard the shouting, and wiping his eyes and brow with one fierce movement along his left arm, brought his cheek back to the gun as one of the whippets ripped past him like a lit trail of gunpowder. He aimed furiously towards the bounding shape of the hare and fired.

The blackness struck him. The wild realization that he had done it again, the blasted gun had hit him again, was swallowed up.

He seemed to have fallen forward and thought he must have gone head over heels. One need possessed him. It drove him to struggle up the hill. None of his limbs belonged to him any more, and he wondered if he still lay in the wheat and whether the cutter blades had indeed gone over him. But loudest of all he heard the dogs. The dogs were behind him with their inane yapping. He began to shout at them and shouted louder than ever when he heard the sound that twisted from his throat, the unearthly thin scream. Then the enormous white dog's head opened beside him, and he felt as if he had been picked up and flung and lost awareness of everything save the vague, pummelling sensations far off in the blankness and silence of his body.

The Suitor

I walk slowly up the hill. It is a black night. Cars sizzle past, and the light rain snows through the beams of their headlights. The surface of the road, the pavements, the low walls, the jumbled shrubbery in the cramped gardens, the iron railings, the gates, the puddles, glisten and glitter like coal, as the wind tugs at the street lights. It is after ten. It is December.

I am warmly dressed, and with my hands deep in my raincoat pockets, in gloves, huddle my garments tighter about me. I feel invulnerable, except for my feet: the soles of my black shoes are too thin. They feel like compressed cardboard. I can feel them blotting up the wet. I bought these shoes for dancing, but I have never danced. I have never even gone to a dancing lesson. Now I wear these shoes when I want to feel smart. Clean shoes make a light heart, a proverb I continually prove. Nevertheless, tonight these soles are out of place. I have resigned my feet to their condition. I have retrenched comfort to a point a little above the ankles.

A wind chopping and cutting and swirling in from all directions throws up the boughs of the elms as I pass under the rectory wall, and swipes my lapels against my cheeks, and clogs my hair with the drizzle. It whips my turnups. It roars among the buildings, and thuds and bumps in the distance.

Here is the house. A truly commonplace house, semi-detached, pebble-dashed, with a shallow defence of imperishable shrubs. Tonight it is merely one half of a black oblong mass. Oily glints determine the windows. It shows no lights.

By day the gate of this house is a dull sooted green, bearing a small oval sign: 'Please shut this.' Its door and window frames are the same green. The lower window of the front room or sitting-room or parlour preserves a cold morgue darkness from year-end to year-end. It is the room in which they lay out their dead. The upper window, or front bed-room, is sealed from the road by the backs of the dressing-table mirrors. Next door, everything is the same, except for the colour of the woodwork, which is a dull sooted red. Even so, the green here is no distinction. In the twelve houses before the next street it recurs seven times. The red is more distinctive, it recurs only twice. Then there is one house brown, and one house black, uniquely.

I am walking slowly, but now I slow down till I move at no more than a saunter. I have seen clearly that the house shows no lights to the front. Perhaps a light shines from the kitchen or side window, but this is difficult to know, because a high wattle fence, parallel to the front garden wall and the road, joins the side of the house to the side of the next and lower house, concealing the side door and kitchen window and the back garden from view of the road. In this fence there is a flimsy door, on the straight concrete path which leads from the front gate, past an offshoot to the front door, to the side door. It is a path I have never trodden, except in imagination. And the door in the high fence, which I have never opened, is shut. I walk slowly, in order to detect signs of light through the chinks of the wattle.

At this moment I am aware of my attention being drawn forcibly in the opposite direction. Since I am peering to-wards the wattle from my eye-corner, without any public show of curiosity, with my face set directly ahead and down-ward a little, I have only to switch my eyes across and I see the figure of a man standing under the wall of the derelict smithy at the bottom of the mud lane, which at that point leads off, an old farm lane, into waste-land and new building sites beyond. For a moment, I make an effort to see him at all, since he stands in the blackest of the cone of shadow protected from the nearest street light by the corner of the stone-built smithy. I detect him as a form slightly lighter than the shadow, and I see or think I see what must be the pallor of a face. Evidently he is in hiding, his feet on the wet earth of the lane. A man merely waiting would surely stand on the pavement, in good light. Why should anyone wait just there, though? Or, more seriously, why should anyone choose just that place to hide?

What other motive should I suspect? I have walked five miles merely to look at this house, merely for the gamble of walking past this gate from which it is her custom to emerge. A calculation that nowhere on earth would I have quite as good a chance of meeting her, even at this hour, as on the fifty yards of pavement either side of her front gate, has brought me five miles with a concentrated mind. The hope of passing her gate at the very moment she chooses to leave her house, and the faint possibility that my hope may be an intuition, one of those precise and practical signals that bring insects over miles, male to female, has brought me this far and at this hour. And have I no rivals?

Is she exclusively my secret? I scarcely know her. I have watched her at a distance, outstanding among three hundred others. Lately, whenever we have met in the school corridors, she has seemed to smile at me. And here I am, hopeful of a beginning. As yet, I have not even spoken to her. So who may he not be? What could he not tell me about her? I see her life may be more formidably rooted than I had cared to anticipate.

I walk up the hill as far as the next side street, and by now I am convinced that he is in ambush—for her. I cross the street. I turn downhill, walking casually, whistling thoughtfully, walking on the outer balk of the pavement, noting again the working glitter of the gutter as the fine rain drains from the black road. I look into a street-light and conclude that this rain, if it were daylight, would seem heavier than it now feels, and would seem much too heavy to be strolling and whistling in. In fact, I now see that it is raining hard. The observation causes me no anxiety.

As I approach the lane I move in towards the inner edge of the pavement, keeping my scrutiny down. I am quite self-possessed, only curious. Not until the last moment, as I draw level with the shadow beside the smithy, do I glance up—as an unsuspecting passer-by might well glance up, catching at the last moment a glimpse of someone concealed in shadow and so close. Immediately, I look down and pass on, and for a while I cannot think what to do, for my suspicions have been confirmed in the intense shock of seeing an utterly white face, under the level brim of a trilby, above the tight gorge of a raincoat buttoned to the throat. A very thin face, it seemed. At such close range, the shadow had not protected him. A very long thin face. What age? He had not been leaning against the smithy wall, but standing clear and in the rain, a foot from it. A face without expression, like the face of a man driving at tremendous speed. He had looked straight at me.

A hundred yards farther down, I stop at the entrance of the rectory drive, in solid shadow, under the spattering, agitated trees. From here, the curve of the road above presents the front of the smithy plainly lit, and I watch the black gap beyond it. I would prefer to be above him, so that I could observe the house too, which is hidden from this point. Rapidly, I set off to correct my disadvantage. A brief detour through avenues and crescents brings me out again at the side-street above the house, and I stroll down three gateways, finally stopping under an overhanging bush, where I feel concealed. I can see the bottom of the farm lane, but no figure: only black shadow. I wait. I will wait here as long as he waits there.

Minutes pass. Cars zip up the hill from the direction of the town, with steaming tyres. The clock beyond the vicarage elms strikes and the chimes fly over nakedly or are muffled away out of hearing as the wind worries them. Eleven o'clock. I hug my garments to me, reshuffling my warmth. Behind me the shrubbery shudders and flinches dismally. I am a black column of patience.

Now it comes to mind that in the minutes between my passing him on my way downhill and my arrival at this position he could easily have left, going either downhill or up. This is an unsettling thought. I had not reckoned on lying in wait for her. To walk past her gate, pleasurably, was all I had wanted. Ought I to move? Ought I perhaps to move down another gateway or two? That would be getting dangerously near, if he is still there.

I will wait here, till the quarter strikes, and if he has not shown himself by then, I will drop the whole business and go home.

I stand.

Lights in the houses opposite go out. One bedroom light there has been burning since I came. The wind jerks and pulls to and fro, and the rain flicks as from a tugged tightrope. Time becomes immeasurably dense and solid, as I begin to feel the patience of the houses and the gardens.

The quarter strikes, concentrating my attention on the black shadow by the smithy. I wait. Now I realize that a figure has already stepped out clear and stands there on the pavement, at the very edge, looking across at her house. I press back into the gate recess, thankful that the house behind me is dark. How amusingly will our situation be reversed if he now crosses the road and walks uphill past me and looks sideways just at the right moment to find me squeezed in hiding here.

I have been ignoring the passing cars. Now a large black saloon coming downhill attracts my notice. Is it slowing? It is slowing, and swinging across from its own side with orange signal in evidence, gliding down, gathering the whole darkness to the blood glow of its brake signals and its rocking stop. I watch, as I might watch a bomb that comes to rest from its astonishing arrival, and lies quiet. My whole consciousness fastens upon it.

She is here. I know it, and as doors on both sides open, and the dim inner light comes on, her appearance is no surprise, the great fleece of hair as she straightens under the streetlights and slams the door behind her. But who is this other, hurrying round to her side of the car, towering over her, adjusting her collar with such familiarity? Ah, yes! I sink, as it were, into the bottom of my mind. Surely this is no more than I expected? Hardly, since she is not yet sixteen, and that car is of a managerial volume and opulence. I dislike what I see, and what I infer. I hear his voice, confident and unsubdued, as he leads her back around the car and on to the pavement where, as I now see, a third figure has appeared and awaits them.

They are stopped in conversation. Without forethought or design, I drift out of hiding and loiter slowly down towards them, as if I were waiting for someone to catch me up. To support this appearance, I half-turn, pausing to look back up the hill, whistling softly to myself.

The three figures are in alarming activity. She flies to the wall, as if she had been struck. I see her tall partner's arm rising and falling, as if he chopped wood. I see the third figure rolling on the pavement, climbing to his feet, falling again, rising upright and falling again, as the tall man's arm administers over him. All this is twenty yards away, in the harsh cold wet shadows. In a few seconds, without a sound, it is over. The defeated one sits up and settles a trilby back on his head. At once I recognize the watcher from the lane-end. He slews and sits at the kerb, back bent low, as if he were spitting into the gutter. I find I have walked much closer.

The girl and her escort have disappeared. Into the house? Yes, here he is again, coming down the path as I arrive by the gate. He shows no visible signs of excitement, only his hair seems perhaps slightly crested, and the street-light gleams on the balding skin beneath it. He is very tall, and his powerfully tailored overcoat, his packing of scarf and great gloves, give him a giant shadow. He glances at me, and I recognize the type of face, I recognize a familiar category of face. Ah, no! I like him less and less, in these seconds. I like what I infer less and less.

He looks around, briefly, up the road and down. I too, in my assumed aspect of passer-by, notice that the extra figure has vanished. As I continue, I hear the gate clack shut and footsteps go back up the path. I walk on, exhilarated and calmed by what I have seen in simply strolling down thirty yards of pavement. Involuntarily, as if to anchor this extraordinary occasion more surely in its setting, I look across the road to the smithy.

The watcher is back in position, in the shadow.

I look ahead sharply, like one reproved from behind. But I cannot go on, I have to look again.

He is there, he is definitely back. As if he had never moved.

Quickening my step, I retread the circuit of streets and after a shorter absence than before am back under my bush, above the house, looking at the black shadow beside the smithy.

Just in time. The tall figure has reappeared by his car, gigantic in the tricky light. For some seconds he stands, inspecting the vistas uphill and downhill, officially. But he is now off duty. The car door slams. The engine cries out, and with a breasting lift of the bonnet the car surges across the road and away down the hill, roaring again in the distance, a warning flung back into the sudden emptiness of the road. For a moment this emptiness is stupefying.

Then like a black cat taking its chance the watcher steps out of his shadow, crosses the road and jumps over the wall beside her gate.

Not to be outstripped, and aware that events have moved into a new gear, I walk quickly down the pavement, yet again, this time close to the wall of the gardens. I hear the dry creak of the door in the wattle fence. Has he gone through?

For a moment I stand. I have only one thought: 'What is this watcher and what is he up to?'

The situation seems already so much my own, I have no thought of breaking free. How am I to get closer?

The faint fancy that she may yet this night be glad of my intrusion gives me a slight smile. But the fancy is in place, for that long thin white face is somewhere on the other side of that door and full of purpose. The memory of that face makes me reckless.

Avoiding the gate with its sounding latch, I slip over the low wall. I reach the door soundlessly, by walking on the garden soil beside the concrete path. Now, like setting a mousetrap, I ease the door open. I stare through the widening gap as if intensity enough could put out feelers to explore the corners of the back garden. I sidle through the gap and stand.

The wind bullying around the house is a help and gives me confidence, for a bowling dustbin lid would be in order. But how can I hope to hear him? His movements are certain to be as cautious as mine, and he may be far more expert. Keeping now to the concrete path, I stalk down the house side, touching the side door gingerly with my fingertips as I feel with my sodden soles for the surface of the path. I am now standing at the house corner.

Incredible! I hold the house where she moves, breathes, listens, is, and yet for fully five minutes have not given her a thought. But I can hear nothing, as I peer into the back garden darkness, nothing but the irregular wind, coming and going.

Has the rain stopped? Just about.

Perhaps he is just around the corner here, within inches of me, listening for me as tensely as I am listening for him. I leave the path, moving out sideways, intending to find the fence between this garden and the garden next door, if there is a fence, and so feel along that to the bottom of the garden. But between house and fence, treading in some sort of loose soil, I am suspended. I listen.

A sharp crack, a heavy weight on a thick stick, from the bottom of the garden, and over towards the middle. I ache with immobility, allowing time for him to recover from his fright. Gradually, moving only when a special press of wind covers me, I move down the side of the garden. Now twigs come against my knees, prickles: gooseberries or raspberries. I crouch slowly, and feel over the soft soil with my spread hands. Is this a path beside me? I did not seek it before, thinking it might be cindered. This is bare hard earth.

Taking a hint from my position, I creep forward on hands and knees, keeping my feet well raised off the earth behind me, all the while staring into the dark till I feel as if my whole head were one baffled eye. That, to my right, seems to be a bower of low trees, bare at this season, or it may be the frame of a rose arbour. Ahead, either a high rough hedge or a thicket. The sudden onsets of wind seem to confuse my sight and my thoughts, and I realize I can do no more till I have another clue. I decide to remain motionless. I am pleased with the stealth of my advance so far. The wind rummages among these bushes with such haphazard abandon, it will take all my attention to distinguish the human sounds from the elemental.

I wait. I listen. I would see more if I were on my feet.

Slowly I turn my head, pressing my cheek to my shoulder,

rolling my eyes into the far corners, till I see the black mass of the house behind me.

Why is it without light? I had expected to see at least a bedroom window lit, however heavy the curtains. Has she gone into a dark house? Is she sitting in the dark?

For some seconds, I hold my position.

The double chime of the half-hour is torn to scraps by an assault of wind, and absorbed by the unmoved earth.

Now I ease the strains of my joints, re-ordering the stresses in preparation for rising to my feet. I want no cracking of the bone-articulations. I ease my whole position. Gradually I transfer weight from my hands to my knees and bring my left knee forward, setting the sole of my left foot to the earth. I am now almost in the starting attitude of a sprinter.

At this moment I freeze. It comes from behind me. It is incredible.

Clear, naked on my ear as if they took form in the very fibre of the nerve, softly popping flute notes!

I express my amazement by pulling a slow, skin-stretching grimace, a contorting leopard-mask, in the pitch darkness. I hold it, as the flute-notes play over my brain.

From behind me, immediately! Whoever is playing must be crouching there, smiling at me as he plays. He has watched my every move, for he has crept up with me step for step, he is playing his flute for the sheer idiocy of our situation.

Again, this time curving my body a little, I turn, slowly, because I may be wrong. I may be still undiscovered.

And I *was* wrong. How did I miss seeing him before? How has he missed seeing me? With his back to me, he is squatting on his heels, facing the house, his trilby bowed forward slightly, moving slightly as the flute notes, in complete disregard for the wind, climb, step by step, step along, climb, step along, descend tossing something, plunge and search deeply over a dark floor, emerge, climb, climb, work at a height, flaking bright bits off. . . .

The house is utterly dark.

I ease back, till I too am crouching on my heels, and I turn slowly, my whole concentration on the flute notes, for their first faltering, and on the brim of his trilby, for its first alertness. Now I could stretch forward and tap him on the shoulder. Gloating, I fumble on the earth for a stone, but all I can find is a twig, a forked nub of twig. Evidence! I pocket it. He does not know I am here.

And now in a kind of inane ecstasy, I writhe up my features again, stretching my mouth wide, making my eyes bulge, like a man laughing at tremendous volume or uttering a battle-cry, but in absolute and prolonged silence, while the flute notes dot and carry about the black garden and climb the wall and tap at the dark window and come circling back to the bowed attentive figure here, not three feet in front of me.

The Wound

'I came back without a hand, but my comrade was devoured'
FOLK TALE: *Two in Search of Evil*

SERGEANT: Keep going, 521, keep going.
RIPLEY: Keep going!
Does he know where he's leading me, that's the point. What's wrong with him? What's wrong with his walk, for instance? what's wrong with his head? I keep getting that—something wrong with his head. But his head's all right. Look at it. His head's all right. Something wrong with it.
What about me, though, eh? There's me too isn't there, and am I all right, am I? Is there any answer to that? What's the answer to that? No time in all this, not now, I'll come back to it, I'll catch a quiet five minutes and come back to it at my leisure. Yes, then I'll stretch out! I'll let my fingers forget my hands, my feet forget my driving thighs. I'll let my head go off like the moon and forget. I'll sleep for a thousand years, I'll forget waking. I'll be forgotten.
What went wrong, Ripley? Something's gone wrong. Some thing. A slight error

in the thirtieth decimal place is having its consequences—every step a multiplication. Be careful, Ripley.

Now it's up to you, Ripley. You're in a bad way, Ripley. You're tired. What's making you so tired? A leakage of information!

I have red hair. Do you now! Where does that get us?

Nightfall. Nearly nightfall. One flower can still look at another but night is in the worm's hole. None of this is right, none of it.

Is this the same as what went before, that's the point. That's the puncture. Where's the puncture? Find the puncture. Because if none of this is the same as what went before—is it the same though? This is this. But is it? And even if it were would I be capable of . . .

I have red wavy hair in one style or another from the crown of my head to the tops of my big toes and I've been that way since I was seventeen and it hasn't cost me a penny, not a penny, in fact I've saved on it. That's the way I am. Was. Shall be. Surely. Can that change? Me, I'm still me. Who's prone? Who's eating earth? Who's forgotten his mouth and eyes?

That sergeant dragging me with an iron ring round my neck and him on a fool's errand without end. Dragging me through this landscape, these seeming locations, and on and on, and I don't want to move.

It's his head that's queer. What's that black mark on his head? Or is it in my eye? It comes and goes. The dusk! Ripley, you've forgotten something. You've landed face upward in this world, stargazer! And what if you do get back home, eh? Even at this rate? You can't sleep there for the blasted clocks! I'm not myself. Tired. Sarge?

SERGEANT: 521?
RIPLEY: Much farther, sarge?
SERGEANT: Keep going.
RIPLEY: Keep going!
Keep going!
Desert. This desert! Walking through this desert all this time, a desert like raw mustard, a windy desert of raw yellow mustard dust, with an immovable sun like 250 watt bulbs pressed lit on to your eyeballs—walking through this desert accompanied by nothing but your feet and ears, staring not round and about because the mirages are like branding irons, they bear direct on your eyeballs, but staring down at your feet, your boots, going —one after the other, going, carrying you—hour after hour, is it any wonder your brain gets to be—a blister! [Laughs] A great blood blister! Bulging out of your eyesockets—prick the blebs and it leaks down your face!
If you've got a face.
Ripley! Pull yourself together—you have nothing but your own parts, no spares available, these have to last you to the

end. With care, with care! What happened?

After all, this isn't desert. I've never seen a desert. You're here, Ripley. Beautiful soft evening. Lovely midsummer trees. Evening of June 22nd, when all the disasters occur. Soft low hills. A lake. That's a heron, gliding. Cool. Take your time. Dew on my boots. Is it dew?

Sarge?

SERGEANT: Keep going, 521.

RIPLEY: But what are we looking for, sarge? I might see it and not know we're looking for it. Eh, sarge!

SERGEANT: Secret orders.

RIPLEY: But who could I tell, sarge? There's nobody else here but you and you know. Don't you? It's getting dark. You might miss it.

SERGEANT: All right. We're looking for a chateau. A white chateau. You know what a chateau is?

RIPLEY: A chateau!

SERGEANT: Keep going.

RIPLEY: A chateau! How does that fit? How does that fit a body abandoned to gravity, at 32 feet per second. . . . I'm still here. You're a soldier now Ripley, a number. If I ever had a home, I'm forgetting it. I'm in the tight black tunnel, like a bullet in the breach, to be blasted into a . . . No I'm not. Not quite. After all, look at my boots. Boots in grass. Grass, grass, grass—sound of a man moving alive over

the open earth, grass, grass, grass, grass!
Me? I'm not myself. Exhaustion? 99 per
cent of my brain is sleeping on the march.
Am I a zombie then? One per cent
awake. That's about one finger awake—
one finger twitching, like a man who—
[*Yawns*] There go my boots down there
—boot past boot and ahead, leapfrog
sidelong. My feet in the boots are travel-
ling asleep, flashing through the grass
and countryside in utter darkness, past
the copses where the wood-pigeons
circle down, past the ornamental lake
with its chalet on the island, its statues
in the reeds, horsemen, nudes, storks
and fauns, past the great oaks over their
wells of shadow where the deer flick
their ears. My eyes are awake here,
travelling horizontally five feet above the
grass, through the midsummer twilight.
Past the great top-heavy oaks, the elms,
the chestnuts, the towering trees at
anchor, in a misty harbour, by a still sea,
waiting, moored by gossamers to the tips
of the grass blades. Trees weighing
hundreds of tons of darkness. When the
gossamers part they'll float the whole
green loaded world away into evening,
the deer stirring, the statues pointing,
the pigeons sitting side by side in the
dark yews, like loaves sliding into an
oven—a top-heavy world slowly tilting
over into darkness.
Ripley. You're Ripley. Not to forget it.
You're the memorable Ripley.

Who's that young chap walking through that parkland with Sergeant Massey? Oh, that's Private Ripley, you know him. Private Ripley, you're a fine figure of a lad, you must weigh twelve stone. Thirteen stone six, sir, stripped to the hairs. Well now, can you identify this one? Red wavy hair, sandpaper skin, a birthmark like a bilberry here behind the left ear, prominent nostril hairs, some grey in spite of his youth, large nose twice broken and giving out a click on manipulation, eyebrows recently burned off, eyes—indeterminate, one gold filled molar, massive neck, heavily freckled forearms the thickness of a racing cyclist's thighs? Hm? Who? Oh, that looks like Private Ripley, sir, in fact it's him for certain.

Me. Ripley, in power. With a headache. Walking.

SERGEANT: Now we bear left.

RIPLEY: Bear left? What does he know about it? I saw him. He staggered to the left, then shouted 'Bear left'.

Watch him. Where is he? Where is he? Sarge! Sarge! Sarge!

SERGEANT: [*Very close*] I'm here, 521, what's up?

RIPLEY: Where were you? I thought you'd dropped down a hole.

SERGEANT: Me dropped down a hole? Wake up, Ripley, wake up. And hurry up. Bear left.

RIPLEY: [*To himself*] It was different. We were—not here. Was it even summer? I don't think it was even summer. Yes, that's a question now, isn't it, was it even summer because this is summer.

Exhaustion. When you're exhausted as I am your brain sort of decomposes temporarily, it no longer fills its circuits, like a fountain turned down. Or turned off.

Rain! That was it—rain! It was raining. I was wet. It was streaming, it was dam-burst, mud and rumble and brown water, my uniform was like a dead skin, I couldn't get out of it, and no leaves, there were none of these leaves, the trees were leafless what there was of them, and there was little enough, they were stumps, stakes, spits and jags—it was forest-fireland, a black downpour moonland, and we were in that farm, we were in that farm, we were in that farmhouse and three tanks, yes that was it—we were in that farmhouse and Joe Moss —Joe Moss was smashing tops off beer bottles against a brick. . . . Wait a minute, wait a minute, get it right. Joe Moss had just had his hand blown off and the blood shot like pop out of a bottle and the rain was hosing down. [*Laughs*] I've got it, I've got it, it can't get away. [*Shouting*] that was it, I've got it. . . .

SERGEANT: Hold on, boy, hold on. Everything's all right.

RIPLEY: [*Yelling*] I've got it——

SERGEANT: Yes, yes, you've got it and very nice it is

now just—there. You're not the first
I've seen go off like that.

RIPLEY: [*Normal tone*] What's up, sarge?

SERGEANT: Nothing, boy, everything's fine.

RIPLEY: Look.

SERGEANT: What?

RIPLEY: Water. A stream!

SERGEANT: Was that there? It's all right though, it
looks nice and shallow. You know how I
know? The path goes straight down to
the edge which means everybody must
cross here, which means it must be
specially shallow.

RIPLEY: It looks black and deep, that water. Is it
water?

SERGEANT: Come on, let's be over.

RIPLEY: Wait a minute. Did you notice how
everything suddenly got darker just
then?

SERGEANT: What's up with you 521? Are you all
right? You're that pale your face is shin-
ing like a lamp.

RIPLEY: That's funny. Your face is all dark and
dusky. I can hardly see it.

SERGEANT: I'm not a pale man, that's why.

RIPLEY: [*To self*] I can't see it at all.

SERGEANT: I'm a high-coloured healthy bloke. Are
you coming?

RIPLEY: We're being watched.

SERGEANT: Eh?

RIPLEY: Far side, near the top of that grassy
slope. See her? She's watching us.

SERGEANT: She?

RIPLEY: It's a woman. It moved.

SERGEANT: You sure it's a woman? Could be a cow

tail-end on in this light. Or a post. An owl flew up on to a post to watch us.

RIPLEY: It's a woman. Call to her. Go on, ask her where the chateau is. Try it.

SERGEANT: Hello Mrs. could you direct us to the chateau, please? Could you direct us to the chateau? Something's wrong with your brain, 521. There's nothing there. There's not even a post.

RIPLEY: She vanished. She vanished as you spoke.

SERGEANT: Oh come off it, Ripley. First I've disappeared when I'm here, then there's some woman where there's nothing, then she's disappeared from where she wasn't—what's up with you? Is there a woman there or isn't there? How are the facts?

RIPLEY: There isn't.

SERGEANT: Right. Now cross and no more funny business.

RIPLEY: Maybe the chateau's up this way, sarge. We don't want to cross over only to have to come back, do we?

SERGEANT: Cross. Orders.

RIPLEY: What if you cross, sarge, and I go searching up this way this side of the stream. . . .

SERGEANT: 521, we're crossing. Follow me.

He enters, wading

RIPLEY: It's icy. My feet are going dead.

SERGEANT: Keep going.

RIPLEY: Sarge it's——

They shout. Great splash

SERGEANT: All right, boy?

RIPLEY: It's up to my chin and I'm on tiptoe.
There must be a trench or a hole or——

Another splash and shout

SERGEANT: Swim for it, boy, the bottom's gone.
Swim for your life.

The sergeant pulls himself ashore

All right, boy, catch my hand. [*Hauls out
Ripley*] That was a surprise. How are we,
Ripley?

RIPLEY: Oh, God, it must be snow water. It's
frozen my guts in a lump.

SERGEANT: Don't be so soft, man, it's only a bit of
water.

RIPLEY: My calves are in knots.

SERGEANT: Here, give 'em a rub. Better?

RIPLEY: It needn't have been like that.

SERGEANT: Can you move?

RIPLEY: Didn't it get you, sarge, at all?

SERGEANT: Didn't seem to touch me. Bit of a chill.
Passed in a flash. It was a surprise all
right though, who'd have thought, eh?
Drowned a few fleas maybe. What's up,
521? What's up? What are you staring at?

RIPLEY: Shh! Behind you. Top of the bank.

SERGEANT: Well, I'm blessed!

RIPLEY: And farther over to the left.

SERGEANT: Another. Are they women? They look
like women. But there's something
funny about them. [*Calling*] Hello
there Mrs. hello! Could you tell us the
shortest cut to the chateau, could you
tell us the shortest cut——

*As he speaks, one of the women laughs, the
other laughs—laughs repeated in the dis-
tance. Silence. A groan. Silence.*

RIPLEY: [*To self*] Who's this lying here? The boot toes are tilted apart and the feet in them don't seem to care. His boots are here like a load of old surplus, dumped, not caring, no pride, carrying on, good as ever. Here's an ankle with these boots. Another ankle. What else? Search. A hand! Empty, like a beggar's, so weary he has to rest his knuckles on the earth as he begs, waiting for whatever heaven might think to let fall, even if it's only rain. Where does this arm go off to so purposefully? A chest. And over the chest to another arm like itself, sloping away to another hand with upward hooking fingers away there in the distance. This lot looks valuable. Somebody lost it? Somebody going to come back for it? A neck. Throat unshaved. Negligence. Neglect is evident throughout. A neck just thrown here in the muck. Somebody's sole and irreplaceable neck, just lying here. Necks! Necks bent glowing under barbers' razors, necks being sledge-hammered in wrestling rings, necks being fumbled and kissed in dark rooms and dim hallways, in shop doorways, empty churches and under bridges and in train compartments and on office stairs. Necks! Search among them. Necks holding their heads up to cinema screens, necks with boils, necks with cricks, necks bunched sweating pork-fat over strangling collars, necks quivering to the creak of cutlery, necks soaring inaccessible over stoles—search among them, count them out. Finished. This neck's not there. This neck's nowhere among them. A neck's got lost. Is this it? With the head on it—the face! The hills on their way to other hills negotiate this small broken pasture where the weather works, small cultivated pasture, small signature of man on the crumbling map of clay bad for retaining impressions, this nose, these teeth that seem to have bitten through hot iron, the lips peeled back over wires, this chin pushing up through the earth's crust, swelling up through the web of earthquake, irresistibly joyful mushroom, dragging its hair out of the depths, forcing its brow into the light, a blunt wedge. And the weather works at it enormously, invisibly, a sky-size smith labouring with a hammer of nothing or perhaps everything, though so far there's no change to be seen, the blows are so vast and skilful. That finger is flickering. That finger away down there on that hand is flickering. It's signalling. It's signalling to the stars—hoping they'll pick up some of its code and some of its S.O.S. and in turn might think to signal to the cities. It flickers. It flickers. It lies still.

[*Shouts*] Sarge!

SERGEANT: O.K. 521. We're nearly there. That's it. See it. Lovely sight!

RIPLEY: The chateau! It's all lit.

SERGEANT: No, it's not lit. It's gathering the last

light of the sky on its white walls which might be slightly phosphorescent though why I can't say.

RIPLEY: Look at those lawns. What a setting for a peacock! Look at all those yew trees: they've been barbered into shapes.

SERGEANT: Eagles, swords, crowns and angels.

RIPLEY: All in black living yew! Sarge.

SERGEANT: What?

RIPLEY: Everything's so still!

SERGEANT: Follow me. Forward.

RIPLEY: It's a ruin! He's leading me up to this place as if it were something important and it's a complete ruin. Where are the windows? Those are just square holes. What's that smashed gap over the main entrance! You could drive a tank through it. A direct hit, dead centre! This is a chateau in its last stages, a war-dropping, largely dispersed to the four corners and the remainder going fast.

SERGEANT: As you'll see, the war's been here before us. It swept over and partly through. A once noble approach is a dump of rubble. Step with care. Probably one shell did this.

RIPLEY: Does anybody live here, sarge?

SERGEANT: What do you think?

RIPLEY: It's too quiet for my liking. What do we do now?

SERGEANT: We knock.

RIPLEY: Well, go on, knock.

SERGEANT: Listen.

RIPLEY: What?

SERGEANT: It's not more than once in a lifetime you

hear a silence as deep as this.

Laugh in the distance

What was that?

RIPLEY: What? I didn't hear anything. Was there something, sarge?

SERGEANT: What's that you've got?

RIPLEY: An owl.

SERGEANT: Dead?

RIPLEY: It was lying here on the steps.

SERGEANT: Dead?

RIPLEY: That's queer.

SERGEANT: What is?

RIPLEY: It's head's gone. And it's still warm.

SERGEANT: Still warm? I don't like that. Let's feel.

Wail, far off

Listen. Did you hear that?

RIPLEY: What serge, what's——

SERGEANT: Shh!

RIPLEY: [*Whispers*] What's going on, sarge, what's going on?

SERGEANT: Keep still. Keep still.

RIPLEY: What's happening? My—My—Sarge! Sarge! Sarge! I can't——

SERGEANT: Oh, Jesus Christ, spare us.

Faint yap in the distance, repeated, comes closer

It's coming right up. Can you see anything, 521, can you see?

RIPLEY *sobs as the yap becomes loud and close, drowning his sobs, till he screams*

RIPLEY: Sarge!

Yaps cease instantly

SERGEANT: It comes right up. It came right between

us. It came right up these steps between us. What was it?

RIPLEY: What was it?

SERGEANT: It wasn't anything. It had no body. I was looking straight at it. It was five feet above the ground—just that barking, floating in nothing.

RIPLEY: Let's get back, sarge. This is no place.

SERGEANT: [*Banging on the door tremendously*]
Is anybody inside there?
Bangs again
Is anybody alive in there?
Silence.
I'll raise their blasted dead.
Banging

RIPLEY: Sarge, the door's opening:
Scrape of door opening

QUEEN: Good evening. You're expected.

SERGEANT: Ah! Good evening. I'm—er—I'm sorry we had to knock so hard, it's sort of— quiet. Well, if we're expected—it's very nice. Well, that's all right if we're expected. We didn't expect——
We thought, you see——
I'm on secret orders and it's a bit diffi- cult to—to——
This is Private Ripley.

QUEEN: Enter.

SERGEANT: Our boots are a bit dirty.

QUEEN: That was anticipated. Aren't there more of you?

SERGEANT: Oh, yes, you'll get them along all right. They'll be here, they're——

QUEEN: Straight ahead. The banquet's prepared.

SERGEANT: Banquet?

QUEEN: Straight ahead.

RIPLEY: Hey, sarge [*whispering*], what's going on? What's going on, sarge?

Baying and snarling and howling of dogs, a dense pack, screeching and squealing of pigs

Sarge, explain a bit, hey, sarge!

His voice is drowned by the animals

Uproar of animals becomes mingled with shrieking laughter of women, turns wholly into shrieking laughter that is now suddenly hushed, with a few spluttering titters

WHISPER: Here they come.

RIPLEY: Sarge, what's this we're walking into, eh, sarge?

WHISPER: Shhh!

RIPLEY: After all, sarge, this is all fancy phoney regalia, isn't it? All this historical pageantry stuff. What's she? Cleopatra the green mummy, what's she all painted up for? I think we're in on an elaborate trap—she's probably a slim officer, it's probably a new commando stunt——

WHISPER: Shhh! [*Silence.*]

QUEEN: The guests. First guest?

SERGEANT: I'm Sergeant Massey, 5 ft. 11 by twelve stone 8, professional infantryman, loving life, liking love, a loafer, no sins but a blank circle where my mother was, no conscience but a mouthful of oath where my father was, chiefly failing in forgetfulness but untroubled by that, concerned chiefly to feed and be cheerful especially to feed. What is this world? I ride on the bowsprit of five seconds alas, my wake is not my care. It's world enough. My twelve stone eight is just five seconds thick. What is this world, five seconds thick? Who am I to judge of its distinctions, draw up claim and counter claim? I am loaded with vegetables and bullocks and my answer is no questions. My hand is my own. My foot is my own. I am——

RIPLEY: Sarge! Sarge!

WHISPER: Shh!

QUEEN: Finish.

SERGEANT: I am——

RIPLEY: Hey, sarge!

WHISPER: Shh!

QUEEN: You are—finish.

SERGEANT: Yours.

> *Outburst of excitement.* QUEEN *raps for silence*

QUEEN: Second guest?

RIPLEY: Me?

QUEEN: Carry on.

RIPLEY: Carry on what?

WHISPER: Introduce yourself.

QUEEN: Some of these ladies can't see you too clearly.

RIPLEY: I'm Private Ripley.

WHISPER: More.

RIPLEY: 1059521, of the 43rd——

QUEEN: You! What are you doing here?

RIPLEY: I came—with Sergeant Massey.

SERGEANT: He came with me.

QUEEN: Do you know where you are?

RIPLEY: No, but I'd——

QUEEN: Hosts!

FIRST WOMAN: They took me with blood dripping off my chin, my mask was blood and went back over my ears and I'd pulled blood up past my elbows and so I was! And they dragged me from the mob and into the Police Station, two constables, my toes slapping the steps.

SECOND: The Coroner attended, fifteen medical specialists of assorted interests.

THIRD: Experimental psychologists of four countries.

FOURTH: Zoologists of five.

FIRST: Bacteriologists of eight.

SECOND: Anthropologists of seven.

THIRD: With a stuffing of sundries, students and attendants.

FOURTH: While the zinc bench on which they stretched me trembled with the thunder and enthusiasm of the journalists under the windows.

SECOND: They stretched me silently, they accused.

THIRD: Bald domes glistening.

FOURTH: Grease oozing among the hair-roots.

FIRST: Upper lips lifting, quivering.

SECOND: Scalpels descending, quivering.

THIRD: What couldn't they expect?

FOURTH: Why, every year dozens disappear, without trace, without a fingernail or loose hair, and these white jackets already had my canines, roots too, reposing in formalin and I was an extremely interesting case.

FIRST: Something of an oddity but significant highly significant.

SECOND: Hardly our type and questionably human.

THIRD: An atavism intact, from the Triassic.

FOURTH: And a very curious instance.

FIRST: My hippopotamus belly was not concealed in the dailies and beside it a list of large-type queries.

SECOND: Vox populi indignation.

THIRD: Portraits of the vanished.

FOURTH: Indications to observe well the elephantine distension of my abdomen.

FIRST: This sack of Gorilla gut was not got gnawing carrots, they cried, and they sliced it.

FIRST: With joy.

SECOND: To numbers.

THIRD: To the Tower guns.

FOURTH: In the name of the law not to speak of humanity.

FIRST: With the sanction of the queen and twelve grey heads selected in the street at random.

SECOND: They sliced me.

THIRD: Under intense illuminations, they were not in the dark, they did not brave the interior unprepared, their eyes followed their fingers inward.

FOURTH: And what did they find did they find what they hoped for.

FIRST: Lusted for.

SECOND: Sliced me for.

THIRD: Did they find the gold teeth.

FOURTH: The plastic gums.

FIRST: The glass eyes.

SECOND: The steel skull-plates.

THIRD: The jawbone rivets.

FOURTH: The rubber arteries.

FIRST: The rings.

SECOND: The remains of their darlings.

THIRD: The toe-nails.

FOURTH: The gall-stones.

FIRST: The ear-rings.

SECOND: The hair-pins.

THIRD: The ear-plugs.

FOURTH: The balls of grey hair and the indigestible soles of the feet of all their vanished mysteriously beloved——

FIRST: And after all that what did they find in my mundiform belly? What did the committee of investigation and public security find? They found three gallons of marsh gas and a crust of bread!

Howls, shrieks of laughter. QUEEN *raps. Silence*

RIPLEY: Sarge——

WHISPER: Shh! [*Silence*]

QUEEN: This first night's entertainments are prepared. We begin with—the banquet.

General excitement, subsiding instantly

After this we pass on to—fun and games.

Giggles and squeaks, louder but suppressed instantly

After that—to the dance.

Exclamations—'The dance!' etc. Excitement has to be quelled by the QUEEN *rapping*

Finally—to sleep. [*Silence*] Will that be suitable, sergeant? You can't refuse, I'm afraid.

SERGEANT: This is—it's—— Well, as a matter of

fact we were thinking more in terms of an old outhouse, you know, mud floors, animals, creepy-crawlies in your ears, that's more our point of view. But this —I'm speechless.

QUEEN: You're hungry. Your mouth's open.

SERGEANT: I could eat a dead horse.

QUEEN: Nothing here but peacock, snipe, woodcock, quail, black-cock, gamecock and cock starlings. Dogfish, catfish and assorted shellfish. Cod and conger, gudgeon and sturgeon, pickled, creamed or else plain. As you please. Eels. Fourteen kinds of duck, a hare, a boar and a roebuck. To your places. Eat.

VOICES: Sit, here, sergeant, with me.

Between us, sergeant. [*Etc*]

RIPLEY: [*To self*] And what about me?

See me dying anyway to get sucked in here as if I couldn't see what it was. Lousy old brothel, all tarted up, that's all it is, I can see that. Straight off.

Is it though? It's not right, whatever it is. Something's not right.

And what was that funny sort of look she gave me, eh? Explain that. What was I supposed to do, what was I supposed to be, eh? I didn't seem to fit.

Something's wrong with that Sergeant Massey, he's been off all night, he's probably cracking. And look at him now. What's his mouth hanging open like that for? Letting those horrible tarts put things in it—ugh!

Stupid lot of fancy dress all this, that's

all it is. She's no more a duchess or what-
ever than I'm a dustbin. Under all that
mass of glittering stuff, she's nothing.
Look at her sweating under that load of
lousy hair—the lengths they'll go to!
Easier just to hang a flag out. Just an old
very used up tart under it all. Her eyes
go off sideways. Her mouth doesn't fit
her face, she can't keep it shaped. She
has a neck like a stuffed lizard. Her
fingernails are black.
You're in it though, Ripley.
Dying for a fag and they shove all this
stuff at me—birds gone black, fish curl-
ing their ends up, fumigants not food.

Laughter

He's at it though, isn't he. Oh, just look
at old Massey there making his bed.
Sleep's all I need, cure me. A bed. Just
a bed. One bed. One bed somewhere out
of the way. Bloody voices! Just listen!
Can-openers.
Don't listen, Ripley, don't look, you
don't have to, you can just sit here and
let them forget you, just sit thinking,
you've plenty to think about, Christ,
yes, haven't I. If I weren't to think
about—— [*Yawns*]
Rain. I was at rain. Somebody hurt. What
was it? I got that. I see. I see. Yes, I see
now. This isn't dew on my boots after all.

QUEEN: Silence.

Silence

Boy. Boy?

RIPLEY: Would that be me?

125

QUEEN: You're not eating.

SERGEANT: Come on, Ripley, for Christ's sake show some manners, you're not in your mammy's kitchen now . . .

QUEEN: Eat.

RIPLEY: I can't eat fish. It—it makes my feet go dead.

VOICE: Feet go dead? Fish?

QUEEN: There's red meat. Eat.

RIPLEY: I'm a vegetarian. Meat makes me dream blood, it gives me guilt nightmares, I get nightmares being eaten by bulls——

QUEEN: Pass him the gherkins. Eat.

RIPLEY: Not vinegar, it gives me green skin, it loosens my teeth, it makes my hair drop out, it withers all my skin up, it brings me out in fungus——

QUEEN: Eat. Eat.

RIPLEY: I'm eating.

QUEEN: Carry on.

Murmur returns: laughter

RIPLEY: Madhouse. And I'm one of the worst. I'm really in it. These gherkins aren't so bad though. How in Christ's name did you get into this, Ripley? And what is it, what is it?

Just look at these whores, faces like earwigs, magnified lot of earwigs. Maggots, writhing, squirming to split their seams —carnivorous pile of garbage if ever there was one. Ugliest pack of bitches I ever did see. That was a funny turn they put on. They learn them off records, amuse customers. Look at Ripley, though, eh. He's away.

126

I'll sneak out of this any minute, sneak out and find a dark room, nice and dark and quiet. Then I'll sleep that long sleep.

GIRL: Come with me.

RIPLEY: Were you speaking to me?

GIRL: Come with me, now, quick.

RIPLEY: I'm all right here, thanks.

GIRL: You'd better come.

RIPLEY: Stop pulling. Can't you see: I'm eating gherkins.

GIRL: Put them down.

RIPLEY: Fingers off.

GIRL: Put them down and come with me.

RIPLEY: No thanks, I know what's good for me.

Jar smashes

You little bitch! They were my gherkins. You've smashed my gherkin jar. Get out. Clear off.

My boots covered with blood and now my hands covered and Christ knows, Christ knows . . .

Rain. That's what I need, rain. This place is too hot. This place is airless. This place is like a tomb in a desert.

She can't have been more than fifteen. And accosting like a desperate sixty-year-old. Little cradle face, it's amazing how it doesn't show even though it's supposed to and even though it does when they get that greasy look at the mouth corners, or where does it show? Something out of sight like a dog-whistle that gets on your nerves and you can't hear a thing.

Something for all tastes in this place. Not for me though. Ripley's bitch-proof. Ripley's dog-poison. Ripley's going to sit here quietly thinking. Explain a few things. Just sit quietly and explain that blood on your boots because it looks fresh.

Burst of laughter

WOMAN'S VOICE: No! No! You couldn't.

SERGEANT: Couldn't? Sergeant Massey couldn't? The phrase doesn't exist.

WOMAN'S VOICE: You ate them! Ate them!

SERGEANT: Oh, Lizzy now, come on, you've trapped mice in your time, what about it?

WOMAN: Ate them though! I get the shivers when I——

SERGEANT: Well, just look at the facts. There we were. Three of us. Three. Not four, not sixty. But three. It was an old farmhouse. Instead of the kitchen we now had a burned-out tank with men hanging down like smoking Christmas trimmings—stopped by this hand. Instead of roof we had sky, full of ghosts just beginning to smell. Instead of floor we had mud and the remnants of friends. Instead of a view we had quag, leafless quag. Between three of us—two Lewis guns. No food. Plenty of ammo. No food. Rain battering down. Three full-utility fighting men, unscratched. I alone, I alone must have accounted for well over well, say at a guess, four hundred of the enemy. Don't stare, think of it. Count it up. One, two three, you, you and you——

bang, bang, bang—four hundred. It takes time. It takes a kind of care. All this time no food. How did we fuel all this personal zest? Were we to be wasted, starved—put under not a new wave of the enemy, resisting formidably, but a miserable hermetic pang in the gut! Principles! Principles came to our aid.

Imagine. These strong lads underfoot—sacks of home-fed weren't they? Oh now, now, now. When you've shot one man into individual bite-size pieces, no ancient prejudice remains whole—everything's holes, anything's holy, if it serves. They served. We served them. Why what would their mothers think, us leaving their boys trodden under that five square yards of undistinguished terrain in neglected postures? Better that we say: 'Lady, I took your son into my own blood and brought him back alive though, alas, killed, but alive . . .'

Shrieks and 'Ahs' and 'It's so exciting'
At the last ditch—and it was a ditch and it was the last—with our guns burning a hopeful circle of survival—for us—like a gas-ring, round us, and the enemy, unnumbered, clutched at the slippery clouds and bellyflopped into the quag, well, look, I'll give you the facts. We cut up those dead lads of ours and ate them raw.

Shrieks, squeals

RIPLEY: Sarge!

SERGEANT: You were there, Ripley, don't look so righteous.

> *Excited murmurs and cries: 'Tell us more, tell us more. What next?' 'You're so brave!' and 'That takes real courage'.*

Courage? Don't speak to me of courage. As if all that hadn't been enough, we seemed by chance and misfortune to lie right in the next wave of not men. They'd got fed up sending men into that porridge. No, tanks, we got next, tanks, in waves. Crawling at us, sawing away at us and fuming and cursing, and at other blokes too you know, we weren't alone quite in this war. Have you ladies ever seen a tank head on, waddling at you, spraying you with red-hot zinc dust and flying earth? No, I know you haven't. Three of us. Flesh and blood. What could we do? Surrender? How? Wave our vests? They were black. So how did we end it? How did we go under? In what way did we die?

RIPLEY: Sarge!

SERGEANT: In what way did we die?

GIRL: [*Whisper*] Come now, quick. Quick.

RIPLEY: Sarge!

SERGEANT: Joe Moss went first. He jumped erect in our pit and started blazing away blindly like a roman candle and that was an expression of his youth rather than of his good sense. But of course he hadn't stood like that ten seconds, not ten seconds, when he went suddenly all calm and still and philosophical—you could see in a flash his face had changed completely. He held his arm up to show us that the hand had vanished. What do you expect? And while he stood like that—well, it's hard to say.

GIRL: [*Whisper*] Quick, now, come.

WOMEN'S VOICES: More, more, give us more. We can't have enough of it. Give it to us. Let's have it all, to the end, to the end. More, more!

SERGEANT: I went next. I wasn't so premature as Moss, but I didn't mourn him long. While he was still moving, a shell hit me here, on the point of the chin. You couldn't see me for mud.

Rising voices drown his—shrieks

GIRL: Now, now, now.

RIPLEY: What are those women doing to the sergeant?

GIRL: Come with me, come with me.

RIPLEY: Sarge!

GIRL: Leave him. He's finished. Hurry, hurry, hurry. In here, in here.

RIPLEY: What sort of a rat-hole's this? It's pitch black. Where's the light, let's have some light.

GIRL: Shh! Be still. Hold me.

Silence

RIPLEY: [*Bursting out*] I can't leave Sergeant Massey like that. Did you see what those women were doing to Sergeant Massey? One of those women had Sergeant Massey by the hair. One had his leg between her thighs and was trying to twist his foot off. His arms were out of

their sockets. What sort of women are
they, are they women?

GIRL: Shh. Be still. Kiss me.

Silence

RIPLEY: [*Outburst*] What's this place? Why have
we come into this room? Why is it
pitch black? Where's the——

GIRL: [*Stopping his mouth*] Shh. Hold me.
Harder.

Silence

RIPLEY: [*Quiet*] Did you see the blood? Did you
see all the blood?

GIRL: I saw it.

RIPLEY: [*Whisper*] Who are you?

GIRL: Hold me. Hold me. Hold me.

RIPLEY: What is it?

GIRL: There he goes, there he goes now.

SERGEANT MASSEY'S *voice comes yelling
towards them, with a pounding of feet,
shrieking laughs of women. Feet and
shouts rush past, as if through the room,
and away like lightning into the far parts
of the house, culminating in a long shriek
of* MASSEY'S *followed instantly by dead
silence*

GIRL: [*As* RIPLEY *begins to blurt something*] Shh.

Silence

RIPLEY: He's been murdered. Sergeant Massey's
been murdered. He's been murdered by
those lunatics and you've been keeping
me in here out of the way and no doubt
it's my turn next. Get your arms off
me, you sly little bitch, off. Sergeant
Massey's been murdered, while I——

GIRL: Don't push me away. Don't push me

132

away. I love you, I do, I love you, I don't want to leave you, don't push me away. Hold me. Kiss me. Love me, love me.

RIPLEY: Get away, get out! Shut up. Shh! I want to listen.

GIRL: Love me.

RIPLEY: Will you shh!

GIRL: Hold me.

RIPLEY: Look, are you a half-wit? You looked quite intelligent out there, have you gone crackers since? Do you have mild fits and funny half-hours or what? Did you hear what I heard? Did you? Are you still there?

GIRL: Yes.

RIPLEY: Right, then get out of my way, because I'm going through that door when I can find it. Will you do as I say and get your hands off. [*He throws her away. She cries out, hurt*] What did you expect? Where's that door! Is there a door?

GIRL: Wait a minute. I've something to tell you.

RIPLEY: Where's that door?

GIRL: I've something to tell you.

RIPLEY: No doubt.

GIRL: You've been shot, you know.

RIPLEY: What?

GIRL: You've been shot through the head. I thought you might as well know. You've a terrible bullet hole right through your head. [*Silence*] There's a place where it went in and a place where it came out, and a tunnel between.

RIPLEY: What? What? [*Silence*] What did they

133

say? Where are you, you girl, you, what's your name, where are you? What's that you said?

He blunders about, falls over a chair, cries out in pain

Shot through the head?

Crazy to say that, crazy to say it. It's just another nuthouse remark, I've been hearing them all night. What about Massey? He was here with me large as life, I've been with him all night, I came miles with him over all those fields and parks and trees and lakes and that black icy river and the lawns and he went ahead large as life, large as life, and he was blown to bits absolutely to bits, disappeared in the air—— [*Shouts*] So it's stupid to say I've been shot through the head, something must be wrong with your brain. [*Silence*] There's nobody but me in this room.

It has padded walls I notice, for the hard cases, you see, just as I thought. Everything's quite simple. This is an asylum for specially hard cases. Now there must be a door because I came in and heard it. There, you see. Everything's normal enough, even here. Quite a nice modern sort of lever-handle. There, and it opens, naturally.

Thick dark as ever. And dead still. That's normal.

Slowly, Ripley. The world is happy. And keep easy. Listen for spiders. The walls, the floor—there's a geographical limit to the size of all these places. There you are, rewards already.

A light. A lantern hanging. Phosphorus. Smell? Stink!

Of all things, a rotten phosphorescent fish hanging on a string, hanging on the hook in fact, just as it was caught probably. What a lantern! Better than a human head hanging without a string.

And it's quite practical, after all. It works. It lights up a doorway.

Door clicks, creaks open

And here we are in the armoury. Or is it a museum? Empty armours, at attention, loyal St. Georges surviving the worm and the virgin, faces open for inspection.

And a candle on a pillar. It glows curiously red. No it doesn't, the candle's not lit. That light comes from the walls, from all over the walls, as if they were faintly crimson, luminous.

Who's this? Sitting, his head in his hands. The Janitor? The nightwatchman, dozing, his head in his hands, his back bent like a man's back bent over the shoulder of a man who has come to rest and kneels and prays. The other listens. Neither moves. They are one.

Sergeant Massey! It's Sergeant Massey! Sarge!

Hey, sarge, wake up, it's me, Ripley. Thank God, I was thinking you'd been pulled to bits by those nutty women. Hey, sarge.

He's breathing.

Sarge, wake up. I thought they were after you, Sarge, I could swear it was your voice, sarge, and I thought they had you too, did you hear that screaming, there was the most terrific scream.

What's he covering his face for? This is the right face, isn't it? It is. It's it. It fought, did this face. Massey carried this face into battle thrust out ahead of his vital parts. What didn't it fight, this face? It fought——

Behind the bomber flights, the dive-bombers, the straffing, the reaping from the air with rockets, the tanks tread-ing, the unsewing machine guns, the big berthas vomiting truck loads of dead high explosive men, the howitzers ploughing and mucking, the field-guns spewing boot-soles and bits of rib, the mortars, haemorrhaging over acres, the flame throwers, the stens, rifles, gren-ades, mines, the primitive tribes of bombs, bottle bombs, jam-tin bombs, glue bombs, boobies, bear-traps, bay-onets, blades of every family and name, with all their bastards and dark horses, maces, francescas bills, pruning hooks, phlegm, turnips, dead sticks snatched up, half-bricks, gravel, clods, fists and invective——

A face.

A face, arms raised, fingers hooked, gums bared, eyes protectively narrowed. A flash, and the flesh flies off that face.

Then it comes on, the glistening grotesque of bone still comes on. A flash, and the visor, the cheek-plates, the girder ridges, the memorial skull-strakes, scatter to shrapnel. But the naked brain, the stripped, grey, stubborn brain, comes on, like a snail freshly skinned, an airborne medusa jellyfish flickering its electrodes, an ectoplasm elemental, a flying malevolent custard!

He was up against it!

[*Whispers*] Sarge.

His brow is sweating. His eyes are trying to open. They can't.

What have they done to him?

What's he doing here, he was blown to bits?

[*Whispers*] Get out, Ripley, get out.

What?

Get out, get out, get out.

[*Runs shouting*] Get out, get out.

Light, light! Thank God, a place with some candlepower. Oxygen, candlepower, and a concessionary pause in time. Where I can breathe. And look. And think thoughts. What's this? Where I can remember words.

> *His voice begins to echo as in a large empty hall*

A ballroom. Spaciously planned, graciously adorned. Scarlet curtains from the gilded moulding of the ceiling to the gloss black floor like waterfalls of blood falling from the bedrooms above. I never before saw a floor made completely of

137

black glass. Unscratchable, unlike flesh. An oiled, impregnable beauty, in a sense. Inviolable, by boot or by boot. Simply silica? A black lake, breathless, diamond hard, without mist or fish, where I stand between waterfalls of blood and look down into my reflection, perfect but inverted. Nothing moves.

I feel terrific! This place makes me feel terrific! It's like the top of a mountain, this isn't air, this is ether. You can slide——

He takes a run and slides

What a slide! This is terrific.

Hello? Company? A gentleman! Excuse me, I'm lost, if you could direct me to the exit . . .

He doesn't answer because he's a dummy estranged from life or the hopes of life. He doesn't answer because all his concentration gathers to keep a needle point of stillness balanced on a needle point of silence, while his violin takes aim on the first far-off, soft, slowly approaching note.

He wears a nice suit I notice, and his carnation is both genuine and fresh. And white. His skin is whiter, shaved within the hour or made of wax. His eye is black. It gleams under its lowered eyebrow like an adder's head in a wall-crevice. It gleams at me, pretending not to.

I see you.

Music. Strike up. Look, you waxwork,

I'm skating over your priceless floor with my ironbound blood-sodden boots—give me some music.

He slides. First bar of a waltz. He stops
What?

All right. Again. Try again. Where's your fiddlestick, you stuffed dummy, I'm raking over your flawless floor at forty miles an hour—that's the way, that's the way!

Violin starts waltz in earnest. Murmur of voices, women and men
Round and round and round we go.

Murmur grows, orchestra comes in, sounds of a full-scale ball

SERGEANT: 521, you haven't changed your boots.

RIPLEY: Sarge! Hey, sarge, are you here?

MOSS: Eyup, Ripley, you gormless bugger, don't stand round out here like a bloody donkey, folk are dancing.

RIPLEY: Moss! Moss, you're dead.

JENNINGS: This is the life, Ripley, this is the life. Get yourself a slice, there's no shortage and all willing: look at this—I just got hold of her as I came in and we've been outside twice already.

Voice passes

RIPLEY: Jennings! That was Jennings. And he died a week ago and the rum I gave him ran back out of his mouth: he had a wound that would have stopped a Bedford truck.

BALDWIN: Out of it, Ripley. What a war, eh? You haven't changed your battle-dress you silly bloody nitwit.

RIPLEY: Baldwin! Not you too.

SERGEANT: Get those boots changed, Ripley, they're dirtying the floor.

RIPLEY: Sarge!

Now, Ripley, just steady yourself, there's a good lad, just take a grip, because if there's something wrong it's here, it's all here.

[*Shouts*] All of you, all of you stop, stop, you're dancing with a lot of dolled-up earwigs, stop dancing you're full of holes. . . .

Dance goes on with slight acceleration

Sarge! Moss! Baldwin! [*He sobs*]

What is it? What is it? It's your head, Ripley, it's your head. No it isn't, it isn't. I see what it is.

He cries out in pain—dance goes on

GIRL: Hello.

RIPLEY: You? Hello. You're not dancing.

GIRL: You hurt me.

RIPLEY: This is my favourite waltz. Shall we dance?

GIRL: I can't.

RIPLEY: I must have lost my temper. I've a very bad headache and what temper I ever had seems to have leaked away. Can you resist this music?

GIRL: Yes.

RIPLEY: What's behind these curtains. I wonder if there's a moon. It was a nice evening earlier on and it should be nearly dawn. Let's go for a walk outside. Me and you. See the flowers stretching and yawning. See the sun come out of its hole.

What was that you said about my head?

GIRL: Your head?

RIPLEY: Look at my boots. That blood's fresh. It's coming from somewhere.

GIRL: Let's go for this walk.

RIPLEY: I can't. I keep getting this feeling it's raining—I don't like rainy dawns. Besides, when I close my eyes I don't seem able to move.

GIRL: Look. Behind these curtains there are french windows.

RIPLEY: This is a craftily designed place.

GIRL: Look. They open.

Sound of storm, wind, rain and gunfire

RIPLEY: What's happened to the trees? They were baled up with leaves, they were full of pigeons, they were fat and full and kneeling under the load.

GIRL: They've been combed out, amputated, cleft, clotted together, pushed over, blackened, abandoned, like the hair of a chewed and spat out head.

RIPLEY: Rain!

GIRL: In its fifth week. The valleys are flooding, the lakes and ponds are brown as old blood, the farms are wading, the dead are loosening from the ground, the cattle are bladders lodged in treeforks. Dead dogs float in and out of bedroom windows. Hillsides are beginning to move. Lost men give up in the fields as in mid-Atlantic. Solitaries sail out to the horizon on haystacks.

RIPLEY: What's that great sky-blinking glimmer and the rumble, like the sun trying to rise. I suppose lots of summer thunder goes with all this.

GIRL: That's your life, working at the hole in your head.

RIPLEY: What?

GIRL: That's the war, working at all the undead. Well, aren't we going to walk?

RIPLEY: Me? Walk out there? I'm not a country boy. I'm getting back in. I'm going to dance.

GIRL: I want to walk. I'm going to walk.

RIPLEY: Out there? Under that?

GIRL: I prefer it.

RIPLEY: Then goodbye.

GIRL: [*Cries*] Come with me.

> *Sudden muffling up of storm sounds, music again*

RIPLEY: Capricious little bitch, wants a romantic walk in the cloud burst and thinks I'm not about two centuries past it.

Narrow your mind now, Ripley, to essential things.

Keep your head very still so your thoughts can roll accurately down into the right hole.

You're very drunk. In fact, you're soused. You're a drowned rat, Ripley, you disgusting person.

Where did you get the drink, eh?

Where's your party spirit? Come on now, get yourself something nice, follow your nose, it's relaxing. [*Hums waltz*] That's the way. See, the headache goes when you do what the headache wants to. All psychological. [*Hums*] This music's a bit fast. No, no, that's your sodden head, Ripley, can't keep up with the world. There now, how about that there, all the trimmings, take that one off, Sergeant Massey.

Hums the waltz which now starts to go slower and slower and heavier and heavier. Cries of surprise and protest turn to cries of pain

What's going on? Why is everybody lying down? I don't know this dance. [*Shouts*] Stand up, sarge, your legs have collapsed. Baldwin, what's wrong? Sarge? Look out, Moss, that woman's

———

It's these women! These women are dragging them all into the ground, it's a massacre. No, they're all sinking together in the black glass, it must have melted with their dancing or the floods have got at their cellars, they're all going under with their women round their necks, with their women panicking and choking their efforts. No, no, no, this isn't glass it's mud and those aren't women and they aren't panicking——

Sarge! Sarge! Sarge!

Growing sound of storm, wind and rain, and rumble of thunder of gunfire. RIPLEY *staggers*

Ripley, Ripley, are you there, Ripley? Yes, yes, yes, I'm here. We're not alone, we're with ourself. And it's raining like hell but we're here, yes, and this mud's only mud, sweet mud, good earth at other times, mother of mankind. We're here. Good old Ripley.

In power. With a headache. Can you move? Move. Move your fingers: look—communications intact. The anger—signals perceptibly, even at this distance. Stand a bit. Maybe the blood'll stop and what if it doesn't? I'll take a draught on the bank. Sway, sway, let the wind sway you, Ripley: oak-tree Ripley riding the punches. All that lovely blood going straight into the ground, it'll grow a nice swede there one day, dried blood full of nitrogen, beneficent. There's a lot of rain missing you that would be hitting you if you were walking.

What a night, eh? What a night to be standing on this bastardly globe of mud in this bastardly sluice, waiting for sunrise. It's a bastard. It's not a bus-stop. The rain's hammering me in. I'll freeze. I'm being driven in like a steel spike. I'll be preserved frozen. They'll come for me after the war, light a fire at my feet. I'll step out fresh, my bed'll be waiting, hot bath, hot-water bottles, hot beer with ginger and brown sugar.

You try moving now, though, just try, just you try, go on, try. I can't.

Oh, Ripley, you've really caught it.

GIRL: Come on, I'm waiting.

RIPLEY: That's that girl again.

GIRL: I'm waiting. You can't stay there.

RIPLEY: I'm hurt.

144

GIRL: Lean on me. Try to walk.

RIPLEY: No, no. What are your shoes like in this mud, I bet they're a sight. My feet are stuck in the mud. We'd better wait till the rain stops.

GIRL: You can walk. You're walking.

RIPLEY: What's your name? Ah, yes, you told me, didn't you. Did you? My memory's been dismantled.

If ever I get back to streets do you know what I'll do? I'll marry you. But we're far out.

I'll marry you. I swear by these boots, by the two holes in my head, entrance and exit, that I'll put my whole body in your bank and you can let me out to myself on an annuity. Will you marry me, though. I'm forgetting, aren't I? That should come first. Will you marry me.

Music ends. . . . Pause
Splashing steps approach

1st SOLDIER: Who's there?

RIPLEY: Old trick. . . . Disappeared. You're a nitwit tonight, Ripley. The world's getting more of a grip on you than you have on it. Is she there? Will you marry me? Don't dazzle there!

2nd SOLDIER: It's one of ours. Look at that head! He's out on his feet. Get him, got him?

1st SOLDIER: Steady. . . . You're O.K. You're in. It's one of Massey's platoon.

2nd SOLDIER: Get back and bring a stretcher up, he can't walk with his head.

Steps splash away

145

They weren't completely wiped out then.

1st SOLDIER: What's he muttering? He's muttering away here.

RIPLEY: Marry me.

2nd SOLDIER: Eh? What's that, boy? You trying to say something? What's he smiling at? Look at this, grinning away as if he'd been crowned. He's more like a drunk than a man with that on his head.

1st SOLDIER: Can we carry him?

2nd SOLDIER: Right. Easy, though.

1st SOLDIER: He must have walked over nine miles with that lot, straight towards us. That's animal instinct for you. Look out.

2nd SOLDIER: Bleeding mud. What a rotten morning. O.K. I've got him.

1st SOLDIER: Keep going.

Their steps splash away in the steady downpour

PART III

Theology

No, the serpent did not
Seduce Eve to the apple.
All that's simply
Corruption of the facts.

Adam ate the apple.
Eve ate Adam.
The serpent ate Eve.
This is the dark intestine.

The serpent, meanwhile,
Sleeps his meal off in Paradise—
Smiling to hear
God's querulous calling.

Gog

I

I woke to a shout: 'I am Alpha and Omega.'
Rocks and a few trees trembled
Deep in their own country.
I ran and an absence bounded beside me.

The dog's god is a scrap dropped from the table.
The mouse's saviour is a ripe wheat grain.
Hearing the Messiah cry
My mouth widens in adoration.

How fat are the lichens!
They cushion themselves on the silence.
The air wants for nothing.
The dust, too, is replete.

What was my error? My skull has sealed it out.
My great bones are massed in me.
They pound on the earth, my song excites them.
I do not look at the rocks and stones, I am frightened of what
they see.

I listen to the song jarring my mouth
Where the skull-rooted teeth are in possession.
I am massive on earth. My feetbones beat on the earth
Over the sounds of motherly weeping . . .

Afterwards I drink at a pool quietly.
The horizon bears the rocks and trees away into twilight.
I lie down. I become darkness.

Darkness that all night sings and circles stamping.

II

The sun erupts. The moon is deader than a skull.
The grass-head waves day and night and will never know it
exists.
The stones are as they were. And the creatures of earth
Are mere rainfall rivulets, in flood or empty paths.
The atoms of saints' brains are swollen with the vast bubble
of nothing.
Everywhere the dust is in power.

Then whose
Are these
Eyes,
        eyes and
Dance of wants,
Of offering?

Sun and moon, death and death,
Grass and stones, their quick peoples, and the bright
particles
Death and death and death—

Her mirrors.

III

Out through the dark archway of earth, under the ancient
lintel overwritten with roots,
Out between the granite jambs, gallops the hooded horseman
of iron.
Out of the wound-gash in the earth, the horseman mounts,
shaking his plumes clear of dark soil.
Out of the blood-dark womb, gallops bowed the horseman of
iron.

The blood-crossed Knight, the Holy Warrior, hooded with
                    iron, the seraph of the bleak edge.
Gallops along the world's ridge in moonlight.

Through slits of iron his eyes search for the softness of the
                    throat, the navel, the armpit, the groin.
Bring him clear of the flung web and the coil that vaults from
                    the dust.

Through slits of iron, his eyes have found the helm of the
                    enemy, the grail,
The womb-wall of the dream that crouches there, greedier
                    than a foetus,
Suckling at the root-blood of the origins, the salt-milk drug
                    of the mothers.

Shield him from the dipped glance, flying in half light, that
                    tangles the heels,
The grooved kiss that swamps the eyes with darkness.
Bring him to the ruled slab, the octaves of order,
The law and mercy of number. Lift him
Out of the octopus maw and the eight lunatic limbs
Of the rocking, sinking cradle.

The unborn child beats on the womb-wall.
He will need to be strong
To follow his weapons towards the light.
Unlike Coriolanus, follow the blades right through Rome

And right through the smile
That is the judge's fury
That is the wailing child
That is the ribboned gift
That is the starved adder
That is the kiss in the dream

That is the nightmare pillow
That is the seal of resemblances
That is illusion
That is illusion

The rider of iron, on the horse shod with vaginas of iron,
Gallops over the womb that makes no claim, that is of stone.
His weapons glitter under the lights of heaven.
He follows his compass, the lance-blade, the gunsight, out
Against the fanged grail and tireless mouth
Whose cry breaks his sleep
Whose coil is under his ribs
Whose smile is in the belly of woman
Whose satiation is in the grave.

Out under the blood-dark archway, gallops bowed the horse-
                                             man of iron.

Kreutzer Sonata

Now you have stabbed her good
A flower of unknown colour appallingly
Blackened by your surplus of bile
Blooms wetly on her dress.

'Your mystery! Your mystery! . . .'
All facts, with all absence of facts,
Exhale as the wound there
Drinks its roots and breathes them to nothing.

Vile copulation! Vile!—— etcetera.
But now your dagger has outdone everybody's.
Say goodbye, for your wife's sweet flesh goes off,
Booty of the envious spirit's assault.

A sacrifice, not a murder.
One hundred and forty pounds
Of excellent devil, for God.
She tormented Ah demented you

With that fat lizard Trukachevsky,
That fiddling, leering penis.
Yet why should you castrate yourself
To be rid of them both?

Now you have stabbed her good
Trukachevsky is cut off
From any further operation on you,
And she can find nobody else.

Rest in peace, Tolstoy!
It must have taken supernatural greed
To need to corner all the meat in the world,
Even from your own hunger.

Out

I

The Dream Time

My father sat in his chair recovering
From the four-year mastication by gunfire and mud,
Body buffeted wordless, estranged by long soaking
In the colours of mutilation.
                                   His outer perforations
Were valiantly healed, but he and the hearth-fire, its blood-
                                                        flicker
On biscuit-bowl and piano and table-leg,
Moved into strong and stronger possession
Of minute after minute, as the clock's tiny cog
Laboured and on the thread of his listening
Dragged him bodily from under
The mortised four-year strata of dead Englishmen
He belonged with. He felt his limbs clearing
With every slight, gingerish movement. While I, small and
                                                        four,
Lay on the carpet as his luckless double,
His memory's buried, immovable anchor,
Among jawbones and blown-off boots, tree-stumps, shell-
                                                cases and craters,
Under rain that goes on drumming its rods and thickening
Its kingdom, which the sun has abandoned, and where nobody
Can ever again move from shelter.

II

The dead man in his cave beginning to sweat;
The melting bronze visor of flesh
Of the mother in the baby-furnace——

Nobody believes, it
Could be nothing, all
Undergo smiling at
The lulling of blood in
Their ears, their ears, their ears, their eyes
Are only drops of water and even the dead man suddenly
Sits up and sneezes—Atishoo!
Then the nurse wraps him up, smiling,
And, though faintly, the mother is smiling,
And it's just another baby.

As after being blasted to bits
The reassembled infantryman
Tentatively totters out, gazing around with the eyes
Of an exhausted clerk.

III
Remembrance Day

The poppy is a wound, the poppy is the mouth
Of the grave, maybe of the womb searching—

A canvas-beauty puppet on a wire
Today whoring everywhere. It is years since I wore one.

It is more years
The shrapnel that shattered my father's paybook

Gripped me, and all his dead
Gripped him to a time

He no more than they could outgrow, but, cast into one,
like iron,
Hung deeper than refreshing of ploughs

In the woe-dark under my mother's eye—
One anchor

Holding my juvenile neck bowed to the dunkings of the
Atlantic.
So goodbye to that bloody-minded flower.

You dead bury your dead.
Goodbye to the cenotaphs on my mother's breasts.

Goodbye to all the remaindered charms of my father's
survival.
Let England close. Let the green sea-anemone close.

New Moon in January

A splinter, flicked
Into the wide eyeball,
Severs its warning.

The head, severed while staring,
Felt nothing, only
Tilted slightly.

O lone
Eyelash on the darkening
Stripe of blood, O sail of death!

Frozen
In ether
Unearthly

Shelley's faint-shriek
Trying to thaw while zero
Itself loses consciousness.

The Warriors of the North

Bringing their frozen swords, their salt-bleached eyes, their
                                       salt-bleached hair,
The snow's stupefied anvils in rows,
Bringing their envy,
The slow ships feelered Southward, snails over the steep
                             sheen of the water-globe.

Thawed at the red and black disgorging of abbeys,
The bountiful, cleft casks,
The fluttered bowels of the women of dead burghers,
And the elaborate, patient gold of the Gaels.

To no end
But this timely expenditure of themselves,
A cash-down, beforehand revenge, with extra,
For the gruelling relapse and prolongueur of their blood

Into the iron arteries of Calvin.

Karma

When the world-quaking tears were dropped
At Dresden at Buchenwald
Earth spewed up the bones of the Irish.

Queen Victoria refused the blame
For the Emperors of Chou herding their rubbish
Into battle roped together.

The seven lamented millions of Zion
Rose musically through the frozen mouths
Of Russia's snowed-under millions.

They perch, as harps,
Over the slaves whose singing blood still flows
Through the Atlantic and up the Mississippi

And up the jugular
Smoulderingly
Skywriting across the cortex

That the heart, a gulping mask, demands, demands
Appeasement
For its bloody possessor.

And a hundred and fifty million years of hunger
Killing gratefully as breathing
Moulded the heart and the mouth

That cry for milk
From the breast
Of the mother

Of the God
Of the world
Made of Blood.

They have gone into dumber service. They have gone down
To labour with God on the beaches. They fatten
Under the haddock's thumb. They rejoice
Through the warped mouth of the flounder.

They have melted like my childhood under earth's motherly
                                                      curve
And are nowhere they are not here I know nothing
Cries the poulterer's hare hanging
Upside down above the pavement
Staring into a bloody bag Not here

Cry the eyes from the depths

Of the mirror's seamless sand.

Song of a Rat

I
The Rat's Dance

The rat is in the trap, it is in the trap,
And attacking heaven and earth with a mouthful of screeches
like torn tin,
An effective gag.
When it stops screeching, it pants

And cannot think
'This has no face, it must be God' or

'No answer is also an answer.'
Iron jaws, strong as the whole earth

Are stealing its backbone
For a crumpling of the Universe with screechings,

For supplanting every human brain inside its skull with a rat-
body that knots and unknots,
A rat that goes on screeching,

Trying to uproot itself into each escaping screech,
But its long fangs bar that exit—

The incisors bared to the night spaces, threatening the
constellations,

The glitterers in the black, to keep off,

Keep their distance,
While it works this out.

The rat understands suddenly. It bows and is still,
With a little beseeching of blood on its nose-end.

II
The Rat's Vision

The rat hears the wind saying something in the straw
And the night-fields that have come up to the fence, leaning
their silence,

The widowed land
With its trees that know how to cry

The rat sees the farm bulk of beam and stone
Wobbling like reflection on water.
The wind is pushing from the gulf
Through the old barbed wire, in through the trenched gate-
way, past the gates of the ear, deep
into the worked design of days,

Breathes onto the solitary snow crystal

The rat screeches
And 'Do not go' cry the dandelions, from their heads of folly
And 'Do not go' cry the yard cinders, who have no future,
only their infernal aftermath
And 'Do not go' cries the cracked trough by the gate, fatalist
of starlight and zero

'Stay' says the arrangement of stars

Forcing the rat's head down into godhead.

III
The Rat's Flight

The heaven shudders, a flame unrolled like a whip,
And the stars jolt in their sockets.
And the sleep-souls of eggs
Wince under the shot of shadow—

That was the Shadow of the Rat
Crossing into power
Never to be buried

The horned Shadow of the Rat
Casting here by the door
A bloody gift for the dogs

While it supplants Hell.

Heptonstall

Black village of gravestones.
The hill's collapsed skull
Whose dreams die back
Where they were born.

Skull of a sheep
Whose meat melts
Under its own rafters.
Only the flies leave it.

Skull of a bird,
The great geographies
Drained to sutures
Of cracked windowsills.

Life tries.

Death tries.

The stone tries.

Only the rain never tires.

Ballad from a Fairy Tale

I stood in a dark valley
And I saw, down the dark valley,
Halifax boiling in silver
A moon disintegrating
In a fury of ghostly brilliance

And climbing out, in a glare of snow,
Pounding to smoke a lake of silver
A swan the size of a city
A slow, colossal power
Far too heavy for the air
Writhing slowly upwards
It came beating towards me
Low over Hathershelf
In a storm of pouring light

And it was no swan
It was a white angel
Leaning into her flight
Gigantic above the moor
Which glowed redly beneath her
An angel of smoking snow
With bare, lovely feet
Her long dress fluttering at her ankles
And silent, immense wingbeat.
'Mother,' I cried, 'O Mother,
I have seen an angel
Will it be a blessing?'
But my mother's answer
Even now I dare not write.

And still the angel lit the valley
And all the moors to the south
Flying toward the West
Slowly, not fading,
And strangest of all
Wearing no halo
But a strange square of satin
I could not understand it
A rippling brim of satin
That fluttered its fringed edges
In the wind of her flying.
Then this enormous beauty
Passed under the rough hilltop
Opposite the house
Where my father was born
Where my grandmother died.
It passed from my sight
And the valley was dark.
And it had been a vision.
That was long ago.

When I next saw
That fringed square of satin
I could have reached and touched it
But I was standing in a valley
Deeper than any dream.
And again it passed from my sight
And sank beneath the hilltop
Opposite the other.

And through my mother's answer
I saw all I had dreaded
But with its meaning doubled.
And the valley was dark.

Skylarks

I

The lark begins to go up
Like a warning
As if the globe were uneasy—

Barrel-chested for heights,
Like an Indian of the high Andes,

A whippet head, barbed like a hunting arrow,

But leaden
With muscle
For the struggle
Against
Earth's centre.

And leaden
For ballast
In the rocketing storms of the breath.

Leaden
Like a bullet
To supplant
Life from its centre.

II

Crueller than owl or eagle

A towered bird, shot through the crested head
With the command, Not die

But climb

Climb

Sing

Obedient as to death a dead thing.

III

I suppose you just gape and let your gaspings
Rip in and out through your voicebox
                              O lark

And sing inwards as well as outwards
Like a breaker of ocean milling the shingle
                              O lark

O song, incomprehensibly both ways—
Joy! Help! Joy! Help!
                     O lark

IV

My idleness curdles
Seeing the lark labour near its cloud
Scrambling
In a nightmare difficulty
Up through the nothing

Its feathers thrash, its heart must be drumming like a motor,
As if it were too late, too late

Dithering in ether
Its song whirls faster and faster
And the sun whirls
The lark is evaporating

Till my eye's gossamer snaps
            and my hearing floats back widely to earth

After which the sky lies blank open
Without wings, and the earth is a folded clod.

Only the sun goes silently and endlessly on with the lark's
                                                    song.

V

All the dreary Sunday morning
Heaven is a madhouse
With the voices and frenzies of the larks,

Squealing and gibbering and cursing

Heads flung back, as I see them,
Wings almost torn off backwards—far up

Like sacrifices set floating
The cruel earth's offerings

The mad earth's missionaries.

VI

Like those flailing flames
That lift from the fling of a bonfire
Claws dangling full of what they feed on

The larks carry their tongues to the last atom
Battering and battering their last sparks out at the limit—

So it's a relief, a cool breeze
When they've had enough, when they're burned out
And the sun's sucked them empty
And the earth gives them the O.K.

And they relax, drifting with changed notes

Dip and float, not quite sure if they may
Then they are sure and they stoop

And maybe the whole agony was for this

The plummeting dead drop

With long cutting screams buckling like razors

But just before they plunge into the earth

They flare and glide off low over grass, then up
To land on a wall-top, crest up,

Weightless,
Paid-up,
Alert,

Conscience perfect.

Mountains

I am a fly if these are not stones,
If these are not stones, they are a finger—

Finger, shoulder, eye.
The air comes and goes over them as if attentively.

They were there yesterday and the world before yesterday,
Content with the inheritance,

Having no need to labour, only to possess the days,
Only to possess their power and their presence,

Smiling on the distance, their faces lit with the peace
Of the father's will and testament,

Wearing flowers in their hair, decorating their limbs
With the agony of love and the agony of fear and the agony
                                                    of death.

You Drive in a Circle

Slowly a hundred miles through the powerful rain.

Your clothes are towelled with sweat and the car-glass
                                                sweats,
And there is a smell of damp dog.
Rain-sog is rotting your shoes to paper.

Over old hairy moors, a dark Arctic depth, cresting under
                                                rain,
Where the road topples, plunging with its crazed rigging
Like a rackety iron tanker

Into a lunge of spray, emerges again—
Through hard rendings of water,
Drowned eyes at the melting windshield,

Out above the swamped moor-wallows, the mist-gulfs of
                                            no-thinking.
Down in there are the sheep, rooted like sponges,
Chewing and digesting and undeterred.

What could they lose, however utterly they drowned?
Already sodden as they are with the world, like fossils.
And what is not the world is God, a starry comforter of good
                                                blood.

Where are you heading? Everything is already here.
Your hardest look cannot anchor out among these rocks,
    your coming days cannot anchor among these torn clouds
    that cannot anchor.

Your destination waits where you left it.

Wings

I
M. Sartre Considers Current Affairs

Humped, at his huge broken wing of shadow,
He regrows the world inside his skull, like the spectre of a
                                                                    flower.

His eyes are imprisoned in the fact
That his hands have sunk to the status of flies.

With skull-grins, the earth's populations
Drift off over graves, like the fumes of a rained-out campfire.

He yawns, tilting an extinct eyeball
To the fly asleep on the lampshade.

Yet his heart pounds on undeterred. . . .

The skull-splitting polyp of his brain, on its tiny root,
Lolls out over him ironically:

Angels, it whispers, are metaphors, in man's image,
For the amoeba's exhilarations.

He sits on, in the twice-darkened room,
Pondering on the carrion-eating skate,

And on its wings, lifted, white, like an angel's,
And on those cupid lips in its deathly belly,

And on the sea, this tongue in his ear, licking the last of pages.

II
Kafka Writes

And he is an owl
He is an owl, 'Man' tattooed in his armpit
Under the broken wing
[Stunned by the glare, he fell here]
Under the broken wing of huge shadow that twitches across
the floor.

He is a man in hopeless feathers.

III
Einstein Plays Bach

And finally he has fallen. And the great shattered wing
Of shadow is across the floor.
His memory is lifting what it can manage
Of the two worlds, and a few words.

The tired mask of folds, the eyes in mourning,
The sadness of the monkeys in their cage—
Star peering at star through the walls
Of a cage full of nothing.

And no quails tumbling
From the cloud. And no manna
For angels.
Only the pillar of fire contracting its strength into a star-
mote.
Now the sargasso of a single sandgrain
Would come sweeter than the brook from the rock
To a mouth
Blasted with star-vapour.

A robin glimpsed him walking,—that was exciting!
But the tears he almost shed went away,
A cloud no bigger than his hand,
A cramped wreath of lightnings, that could not find the earth.

He bows in prayer over music, as over a well.
But it is the cauldron of the atom.
And it is the Eye of God in the whirlwind.
It is a furnace, storming with flames.

It is a burned-out bottomless eye-socket
Crawling with flies
In fugues
And he prays

'Mother! Mother!
                    O mother

Send me love.'

                    But the flies

The flies rise in a cloud.

Pibroch

The sea cries with its meaningless voice
Treating alike its dead and its living,
Probably bored with the appearance of heaven
After so many millions of nights without sleep,
Without purpose, without self-deception.

Stone likewise. A pebble is imprisoned
Like nothing in the Universe.
Created for black sleep. Or growing
Conscious of the sun's red spot occasionally,
Then dreaming it is the foetus of God.

Over the stone rushes the wind
Able to mingle with nothing,
Like the hearing of the blind stone itself.
Or turns, as if the stone's mind came feeling
A fantasy of directions.

Drinking the sea and eating the rock
A tree struggles to make leaves——
An old woman fallen from space
Unprepared for these conditions.
She hangs on, because her mind's gone completely.

Minute after minute, aeon after aeon,
Nothing lets up or develops.
And this is neither a bad variant nor a tryout.
This is where the staring angels go through.
This is where all the stars bow down.

The Howling of Wolves

Is without world.

What are they dragging up and out on their long leashes of
sound
That dissolve in the mid-air silence?

Then crying of a baby, in this forest of starving silences,
Brings the wolves running.
Tuning of a violin, in this forest delicate as an owl's ear,
Brings the wolves running—brings the steel traps clashing
and slavering,
The steel furred to keep it from cracking in the cold,
The eyes that never learn how it has come about
That they must live like this,

That they must live

Innocence crept into minerals.

The wind sweeps through and the hunched wolf shivers.
It howls you cannot say whether out of agony or joy.

The earth is under its tongue,
A dead weight of darkness, trying to see through its eyes.
The wolf is living for the earth.
But the wolf is small, it comprehends little.

It goes to and fro, trailing its haunches and whimpering
horribly.
It must feed its fur.

The night snows stars and the earth creaks.

Gnat-Psalm

'The Gnat is of more ancient lineage than man.'   *Proverb.*

When the gnats dance at evening
Scribbling on the air, sparring sparely,
Scrambling their crazy lexicon,
Shuffling their dumb Cabala,
Under leaf shadow

Leaves only leaves
Between them and the broad thrusts of the sun
Leaves muffling the dusty stabs of the late sun
From their frail eyes and crepuscular temperaments

Dancing
Dancing
Writing on the air, rubbing out everything they write
Jerking their letters into knots, into tangles
Everybody everybody else's yoyo

Immense magnets fighting around a centre

Not writing and not fighting but singing
That the cycles of this Universe are no matter
That they are not afraid of the sun
That the one sun is too near
It blasts their song, which is of all the suns
That they are their own sun
Their own brimming over
At large in the nothing
Their wings blurring the blaze
Singing
Singing

That they are the nails
In the dancing hands and feet of the gnat-god
That they hear the wind suffering
Through the grass
And the evening hill suffering
And the towns, camped by their graveyards,
Saddening into an utter darkness

The wind bowing with long cat-gut cries
And highways and airways
Dancing in the wind
The wind's dance, the death-dance,
Plunging into marshes and undergrowth
And cities like cowdroppings huddling to dust

But not the gnats, their agility
Has outleaped that threshold
And hangs them a little above the claws of the grass
Dancing
Dancing
In the glove shadows of the sycamore

A dance never to be altered
A dance giving their bodies to be burned

And their mummy faces will never be used

Their little bearded faces
Weaving and bobbing on the nothing
Shaken in the air, shaken, shaken
And their feet dangling like the feet of victims

O little Hasids
Ridden to death by your own bodies
Riding your bodies to death
You are the angels of the only heaven!

And God is an Almighty Gnat!
You are the greatest of all the galaxies!
My hands fly in the air, they are follies
My tongue hangs up in the leaves
My thoughts have crept into crannies

Your dancing

Your dancing

Rolls my staring skull slowly away into outer space.

Full Moon and Little Frieda

A cool small evening shrunk to a dog bark and the clank of a
bucket—

And you listening.
A spider's web, tense for the dew's touch.
A pail lifted, still and brimming—mirror
To tempt a first star to a tremor.

Cows are going home in the lane there, looping the hedges
with their warm wreaths of breath—
A dark river of blood, many boulders,
Balancing unspilled milk.

'Moon!' you cry suddenly, 'Moon! Moon!'

The moon has stepped back like an artist gazing amazed at a
work
That points at him amazed.

Wodwo

What am I? Nosing here, turning leaves over
Following a faint stain on the air to the river's edge
I enter water. What am I to split
The glassy grain of water looking upward I see the bed
Of the river above me upside down very clear
What am I doing here in mid-air? Why do I find
this frog so interesting as I inspect its most secret
interior and make it my own? Do these weeds
know me and name me to each other have they
seen me before, do I fit in their world? I seem
separate from the ground and not rooted but dropped
out of nothing casually I've no threads
fastening me to anything I can go anywhere
I seem to have been given the freedom
of this place what am I then? And picking
bits of bark off this rotten stump gives me
no pleasure and it's no use so why do I do it
me and doing that have coincided very queerly
But what shall I be called am I the first
have I an owner what shape am I what
shape am I am I huge if I go
to the end on this way past these trees and past these trees
till I get tired that's touching one wall of me
for the moment if I sit still how everything
stops to watch me I suppose I am the exact centre
but there's all this what is it roots
roots roots roots and here's the water
again very queer but I'll go on looking

Acknowledgements

Acknowledgements are due to the editors of the following publications, in which these poems and stories have appeared: *Agenda, Atlantic Monthly, Critical Quarterly, Encounter, Harper's Bazaar, The Listener, The London Magazine, The New Statesman, The New York Review of Books, The New Yorker,* and the *Observer.*

'The Rain Horse', 'Sunday' and 'Snow' originally appeared in INTRODUCTION published by Faber and Faber.

'The Wound' was first broadcast by the BBC on the third Programme on 1st February 1962. It was produced by Douglas Cleverdon with music by Alexander Goehr.